San Francisco

YERBA BUENA

D0702255

Cover Illustration

Yerba Buena, 1846–1847
by William F. Swasey
From a lithograph published in 1886 by the
Bosqui Engraving and Printing Co.

The key to the illustration: A, U.S.S. *Portsmouth*. B, U.S. transport ships *Loo Choo, Susan Drew,* and *Thomas H. Perkins.* C, ship *Vandalia,* a merchant-man consigned to Howard & Mellus. D, coasting schooner. E, launch *Luce,* belonging to James Lick. 1, Custom House. 2, Calaboose. 3, School House. 4, Alcalde's Office. 5, City Hotel, owned by William A. Leidesdorff. 6, Portsmouth Hotel. 7, William H. Davis store. 8, Howard & Mellus store. 9, The old Hudson's Bay Company building. 10, Samuel Brannan's residence. 11, William A. Leidesdorff's cottage. 12, First residence of the Russ family. 13, John Sullivan residence. 14, Peter T. Sherback residence. 15, Juan C. Davis residence. 16, G. Reynolds residence. 17, A. J. Ellis boarding house. 18, Fitch & McKurley building. 19, Jean J. Vioget residence. 20, John Fuller residence. 21, Jesus Noe residence. 22, Juan N. Padilla residence. 23, A. A. Andrew residence. 24, Capt. Antonio Ortega residence. 25, Francisco Cacerez residence. 26, William S. Hinckley residence. 27, Gen. Mariano G. Vallejo building. 28, C. L. Ross building. 29, mill. 30, John Paty's adobe building. 31, Dr. E. P. Jones residence. 32, Robert Ridley residence. 33, *Los Pechos de la Chola* [Breasts of the Indian girl] (Twin Peaks). 34, Lone Mountain. 35, Sill's blacksmith shop. → Trail to the Presidio. ← Trail to the Mission.

San Francisco
YERBA BUENA

From the Beginning to the Gold Rush
1769–1849

Compiled and Edited by
Peter Browning

GREAT WEST BOOKS   LAFAYETTE, CALIFORNIA

Copyright © 1998 by Peter Browning
All Rights Reserved

Cover design by Larry Van Dyke

Manufactured in the United States of America

Library of Congress Cataloging-in-Publication Data

San Francisco/Yerba Buena : from the beginning to the Gold Rush,
    1769–1849 /compiled and edited by Peter Browning.
        p.   cm.
    Includes bibliographical references and index.
    ISBN 0–944220–08–8 (pbk. : alk. paper)
    1. San Francisco (Calif.)—History—Sources. 2. San Francisco Bay
(Calif.)—History—Sources. I. Browning, Peter, 1928–
F869.S357S35   1998
979.4'6—dc21   98–10155

Great West Books
P.O. Box 1028
Lafayette, CA 94549
Phone & Fax: (925) 283-3184

Contents

Maps and Illustrations

Preface

It is my intention in this book to relate a concise history of San Francisco Bay and of the village of Yerba Buena, which would become San Francisco—from the discovery of the bay in 1769 to the Gold Rush in 1849. The history of this era has been told many times, often in exhaustive detail, especially concerning the political and religious struggles that consumed the energies of the Spanish and Mexicans in the pre-American period. I have deliberately compiled a record of a different sort, one that portrays, in words, maps, and illustrations, the impressions, attitudes, and geographical knowledge of the observers of the farthest reaches of New Spain, Mexico, and the onset of the American dominion, as they perceived it over a stretch of eighty years.

It is told as much as possible in the words of the explorers, visitors, and early inhabitants. These excerpts are taken mainly from their published works, but also—in the Yerba Buena period—from newspapers and reminiscent accounts. Most of the unwitting contributors to this volume were selected not only for their words, but also because most of them created maps and illustrations of the bay; and, later, produced the first surveys of the town of Yerba Buena and the city of San Francisco.

Acknowledgements and Sources

I am indebted to many kind, knowledgeable, generous people in the Bancroft Library for their unstinting advice and assistance in helping me acquire the majority of the maps and other illustrations in this book. In particular: Walter Brem, Peter Hanss, Bonnie Hardwick, Richard Ogar, Bill Roberts, and Susan Snyder.

The illustrations on pages 101, 174, and 183 are from Malcolm E. Barker.

The excerpts from Font's diary on pages 34, 35, and 36, and the back cover illustration of Yerba Buena in 1849, are from the editor's collection.

The map on page 142 is courtesy of the California Historical Society.

The maps on pages 85, 88, 109, and 138 are from the University of California at Berkeley Map Library.

All other maps and illustrations are: Courtesy, the Bancroft Library.

Introduction

We are constantly told that we are living in a revolutionary age, and that this is a unique period in our history—and we do not doubt the ferocious evidence of unceasing rapid change nor deny our personal reactions to the daily stimuli. Yet at various times in our national existence our political, religious, and social leaders have claimed that *those* times were a revolutionary age—and what a wondrous thing it was! Progress means change—change is progress—always and forever a cause for celebration.

Each generation since the founding of the Republic has asserted that it is at the forefront of modernity, innovation, and limitless improvement. Built into that assertion is the notion that no generation before it has ever experienced such radical change, such drastic upheaval, such shattering of mores. And how proud each generation is at having transcended the pedestrian ways of its forefathers, and having surpassed the trivial and mawkish advancements of which *they* were so proud.

The acceleration of history is not a recent phenomenon. Wars, revolutions, and mass migrations have occurred throughout human history, and doubtless those alive at the time felt overwhelmed by the shock of events and the rapidity of change. But the speed of change—or progress, if such it be—is not constant. There have been times and places when not much of anything happened, when the advance of 'civilization' came to a halt for decades and even centuries, leaving historians of the future with nothing to report.

Such a place was California before 1769. In the early 1520s Hernando Cortés sent ships north along the Pacific coast in search of the fabled Strait of Anián. There was no such thing to be found, but the 800-mile-long peninsula now named Baja California was discovered. The land was a desert, the Indians hostile, and with political problems brewing at home, Cortés gave up the effort to further expand the boundaries of New Spain.

Juan Rodríguez Cabrillo, another sea captain questing after the Strait of Anián, landed at what is now San Diego in 1542. He also visited Santa Catalina Island and the islands in the Santa Barbara Channel. The next to touch upon California was Sebastián Rodríguez Cermeño, who in 1595 was looking for a safe port where the Manila galleons could refit after the arduous voyage from the Philippine Islands en route to Acapulco. He located Drakes Bay (Drake had been there in 1579), which he named San Francisco Bay—a name that created much confusion during the first few years after the discovery of the present San Francisco Bay. Cermeño's ship, the *San Agustin,* was wrecked in a storm while in Drakes Bay, and went to the bottom. Cermeño and his crew eventually got back to Mexico in an open launch—an heroic journey that saved their lives but had no effect whatsoever on the course of history.

In 1602 and 1603 Sebastián Vizcaíno explored the California coast as far north as Cape Mendocino. He stopped briefly at San Diego, and gave it its present name. His major contribution to geographical knowledge was the discovery of Monterey Bay, in January 1603. The irony of the discovery was that his glowing description of the bay was so profound that the first Spanish land expedition to reach it—an astonishing 166 years later—simply didn't recognize it when they stood on its shores. They thought that Monterey Bay might be farther north, so they pressed on up the coast—and in early November 1769 discovered San Francisco Bay. It is after this great historical hiatus that the modern history of San Francisco Bay begins.

The progress of Spanish settlement of the bay and its environs was slow and halting. The mission and presidio that were established on the future site of San Francisco, in 1776, began to deteriorate and crumble almost as soon as they had been created. George Vancouver, captain of the first non-Spanish ship to enter San Francisco Bay, in 1792, commented on the feebleness and fragility of the Spanish effort—as did practically all the other foreign visitors for the next fifty years.

It was but eighty years from the discovery of San Francisco Bay in 1769 to the magical year of 1849. If one were to demonstrate the economic and social advance of the region on a graph, the line of progress would barely struggle upward from zero—and would even decline at times, to show, perhaps, the high mortality among the Indians, or the collapse of the mission system. The line would show a modest but steady ascent in the early 1840s and up to 1847. By the middle of that year, San Francisco had a population of 459.

Gold was discovered in January 1848, and by 1849 the line would be off the chart at an almost vertical angle. At the end of 1849 the estimated population of San Francisco was 40,000, and 4,000 immigrants were arriving by sea every month.

Now there is a true acceleration of history—a revolutionary age to put ours in the shade.

Ensign Miguel Costansó (fl. 1769–1811) was the engineer with the Portolá expedition of 1769–1770, which discovered San Francisco Bay—quite by accident. The expedition—the first Europeans to explore by land in what is now California—set out from San Diego on July 14, 1769 with the intention of marching up the coast to Monterey Bay, where a mission and a presidio were to be established.

When they reached Monterey Bay, in early October, they did not recognize it for what it was. They had expected to find a snug harbor protected from the wind, but saw a vast roadstead. Thinking that Monterey Bay still lay ahead, the expedition continued north. On November 2 some of the expedition's hunters saw San Francisco Bay from atop a hill, and the rest of the party saw it two days later from what is now named Sweeney Ridge.

Diary of Miguel Costansó

The Portolá Expedition of 1769–1770

Wednesday, 1 November.—Some had not yet been convinced that we had left the port of Monterey behind, nor would they believe that we were at the port of San Francisco.[1] Our commander ordered the scouts to set out to examine the land for a certain distance, and gave them three days within which to return, hoping that from this exploration they would, perhaps, bring back information that would remove the perplexity of the incredulous.

From the coast or inner shore on the south of the bay,[2] the Farallones were sighted west by southwest; the Punta de los Reyes, west sixteen degrees northwest, and some ravines with white cliffs, farther in, northwest by west.[3]

Thursday, 2 November.—Several of the soldiers requested permission to go hunting, since many deer had been seen. Some of them went quite a long way from the camp and reached the top of the hills, so that they did not return until after nightfall. They said that to the north of the bay they had seen an immense arm of the sea or estuary, which extended inland as far as they could see, to the southeast; that they had seen some beautiful plains studded with trees; and that from the columns of smoke they had

---

1. This is actually what we now know as Drakes Bay. Cermeño applied the name of "Bay of San Francisco" to this 'haven' when his ship, the *San Agustín*, was driven ashore here and wrecked during a storm on November 30, 1595. In this instance, Costansó has applied the name to the entire bay or gulf between the Golden Gate and the Farallones.
2. From their campsite near the mouth of San Pedro Creek.
3. Bolinas Bay.

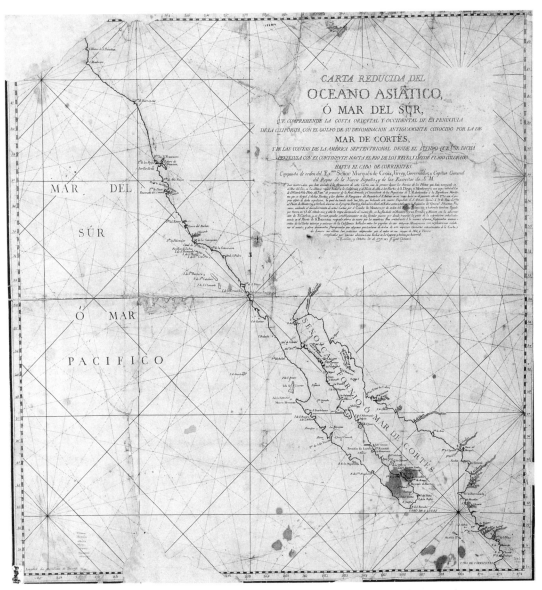

Map of the west coast of California and Baja California, by Miguel Costanó, 1771.
This is the first chart or map to show San Francisco Bay.
(The first version of this map, in 1770, did not show the bay;
the date on this map is still 1770. See the enlargement on the back cover.)

Carta Reducida del Oceano Asiático, ó Mar del Sur, que comprehende la costa oriental y occidental de la península de la California, con el golfo de su denominacion antiguamente conocido por la de Mer de Cortés, y de las costas de la América Septentrional desde el isthmo que un dicha peninsula con el continente hasta el Rio de los Reyes, y desde el Rio Colorado hasta el Cabo de Corrientes. Compuesta de orden del Exmo. Señor Marqués de Croix, Virrey, Governador, y Capitan General del Reyno de la Nueva España, y de los exercitos de S. M. . . . Mexico, y octubre 30 de 1770. Miguel Costansó.

Basic map of the Asian Ocean, or Southern Sea, which includes the eastern and western coasts of the California peninsula, with the gulf having the well known ancient name of the Sea of Cortés, and the northern coasts of America, from the isthmus which is said to be a peninsula with the continent to the Kings River, and from the Colorado River to Cape Corrientes. By the order of His Excellency Señor Marqués de Croix, Viceroy, Governor, and Captain General of the King of New Spain, and of His Majesty's Army . . . . City of Mexico, October 30, 1770. Miguel Costansó. (Size of the original, 72 x 82 cm.)

noticed all over the level country, there was no doubt that the land must be well populated with natives. This ought to confirm us more and more in the opinion that we were at the port of San Francisco, and that this was the estuary of which the pilot Cabrera Bueno spoke; we had seen its entrance between some ravines while descending the slope of the bay. In regard to this, in his sailing directions, Cabrera Bueno uses the following words: "Through the middle ravine, an estuary of salt water enters without any breakers; coming in, you will find friendly Indians, and you will easily obtain fresh water and firewood."[4]

We also conjectured from these reports that the scouts could not have passed to the opposite side of the bay, as it was no mere three days' undertaking to make the detour rounding an estuary, the extent of which was greatly enlarged upon to us by the hunters.

Friday, 3 November.—During the night the scouts returned to camp, firing salutes with their arms. They had kept us in a state of great expectation until we all went out to meet them on the road and began to satisfy our curiosity by asking questions and hearing their answers.

The reason for their demonstration of joy was none other than that they had inferred from the ambiguous signs of the natives that two days' march from the place at which they had arrived there was a port and a vessel in it. Upon this simple conjecture some of them had finally persuaded themselves that they were at Monterey, and they had no doubt that the packet *San Joseph* was awaiting us at that place.

Saturday, 4 November.—We went out in search of the port. We followed the south shore or beach of San Francisco until we entered the mountain range to the northeast. From the summit of this range we saw the magnificent estuary, which stretched toward the southeast. We left it on our left hand, and, turning our backs on the bay, advanced to the south-southeast, through a canyon in which we halted at sunset.[5] We traveled for two leagues.

Sunday, 5 November.—We followed the coast of the estuary, although

---

4. Cabrera Bueno described Drakes Bay and Drakes Estero. The leaders of the Portolá expedition were quite confused in believing that he was referring to our present San Francisco Bay—which they thought of as an estuary.

5. The expedition followed the obvious natural route—the San Andreas Rift Zone—and camped at a pond or lagoon that is now covered by San Andreas Lake.

we did not see it because we were separated from it by the low hills of the canyon that we were following in a south-southeasterly direction. We traveled for three leagues. The country was pleasant. The hills west of the canyon were crowned with savins, low live oaks, and other smaller trees. There was sufficient pasture. We halted on the bank of a stream of good water.[6] Some of the natives were seen; they invited us to go their villages, and offered us their presents of seeds and fruits.

Monday, 6 November.—Without leaving this canyon we marched, in the same direction, for three more leagues over ever more pleasant land, and more thickly covered with savins, white oaks, and live oaks loaded with acorns. Two very numerous bands of Indians met us on the road with presents of pinole and some large trays of white atole, which supplied in large measure the needs of our men. These natives requested us earnestly to go to their villages, offering to entertain us as well; they were disappointed because we would not yield to their solicitations. Some of the men asked them various questions by means of signs, in order to obtain from them information they desired, and they were very well satisfied with the grimaces and the ridiculous and vague gestures with which the natives responded—a pantomime from which, truly, one could understand very little, and the greater part of the men understood nothing. Meanwhile we arrived at the end of the canyon where the hilly country, which extended to our left and lay between us and the estuary, terminated. At the same time the hills on our right turned towards to the east, and closed the valley that contained the waters of the estuary. We likewise directed our course to the east. We proceeded for a short stretch in this direction and halted on the bank of a deep stream, which descended from the mountain range and flowed precipitately to the calm waters of the estuary.[7]

---

6. This location is now under the waters of the Upper Crystal Springs Reservoir.
7. San Francisquito Creek in Menlo Park. This was the high-water mark of the Portolá expedition. The main body of the expedition stayed at this place while a group of scouts went southeast, around the bottom of the bay and up the east side as far as present-day Hayward or San Lorenzo. On their return, they stated to Portolá that there was another immense estuary to the north (San Pablo Bay) and that they would not be able to get around it given the strictures of time and food. When the scouts returned, the expedition at once started out to retrace its steps to San Diego.

The Portolá Expedition discovers San Francisco Bay.
(From a painting by Walter Francis.)

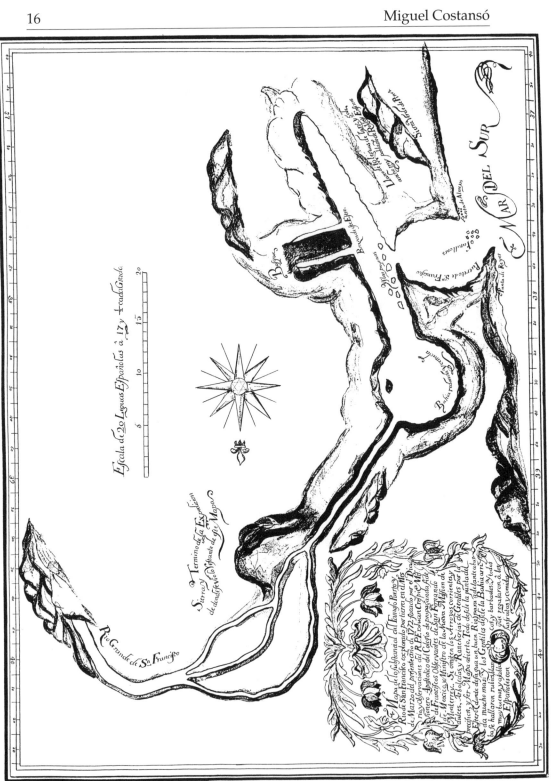

Juan Crespí's map of the San Francisco Bay region, 1772.

Fray Juan Crespí was one of the two padres with the Portolá expedition of 1769. In 1772 he was with Pedro Fages on the expedition up the east side of the bay, through present Alameda and Contra Costa counties and to the San Joaquin River. He combined his personal knowledge of the area with the existing confusion about the regional geography, and produced this peculiar representational map. It is, nevertheless, the first map of San Francisco Bay. (The top of the map is East.) Theodore E. Treutlein, in his book *San Francisco Bay: Discovery and Colonization, 1769–1776,* presents a convincing case that this so-called Crespí map was actually drawn by Fray Rafael Verger or perhaps by Fray Pablo Font, from Crespí's diary and notes. It seems certain that the map was drawn by someone who had not actually seen San Francisco Bay.

The name "Puerto de Sn. Francisco" was the early name for Drakes Bay, at Point Reyes. The seven Farallones guard the entrance to the Golden Gate, and the "small islands" within the bay are lined up in a row. San Pablo Bay is called "Bahia redonda," and present San Francisco Bay is unnamed. On the East Bay coast, the two "Arms of the Estuary" are San Antonio Creek (now the Oakland harbor and estuary) and San Leandro Creek. "Rio Grande de Sn. Francisco" (the San Joaquin) pours forth from the Sierra and becomes three rivers, which apparently indicate the multiple channels and islands in the Sacramento Delta.

The text on the map reads:

Mapa de lo substancial del Famoso Puerto y Rio de San Francisco explorado por tierra en el Mes de Marzo del presente año de 1772 sacado por el Diario, y observaciones del R. P. Fr. Juan Crespi, Missionero Apostolico del Colegio de propaganda fide de Franciscos Observantes de San Fernando de Mexico, y Ministro de la Nueva Mission de Monterrey. Se omiten los arroyos corrientes, y dulces, arboledas, y rancherias de Gentiles por la precision, y ser Mapa abierto. Todo desde la punta del Estero (donde desagua un buen Rio) para adelante abunda mucho mas: Y los Gentiles desde la Bahia arriba se hallaron rubios blancos, y barbados: Y todos muy buenos, y afables que regalaron â los Españoles con sus frutas y comidas.

Map of the essential details of the Famous Port and River of San Francisco explored by land in the month of March in the present year of 1772, taken from the diary and observations of the R[everend] P[adre] Fr[ay] Juan Crespi, Apostolic Missionary of the Franciscans' College of propaganda of the faith, Observants of San Fernando of Mexico, and Minister of the New Mission of Monterrey. Omitted are flowing, fresh-water streams, groves of trees, and Indian Rancherias, out of necessity and for purposes of clarity. From the end of the estuary (into which a fine river empties) and beyond there are many heathen everywhere; and the heathen of the upper bay were fair-haired, white-skinned, and bearded:[8] And all were very kind and friendly and regaled the Spaniards with their fruit and food.

---

8. This is a most unlikely description of any of the Indians of the Bay Area, but that's what it says. Perhaps it is further confirmation that the compiler of the map was working from the diary and notes of someone else, and misread or misinterpreted what was written.

José de Cañizares (fl. 1769–90) was the pilot on the *San Carlos*, commanded by Juan Manuel de Ayala—the first ship to enter San Francisco Bay, in 1775. Cañizares explored the bay in the ship's boat during the weeks that the *San Carlos* was anchored at Angel Island. He produced a map of the bay that year, and a revised version of it in 1776 after a second voyage to the bay. (*See page 22.*)

In 1781 a new version was actually published; the first two had wound up in the archives. Perhaps the most significant aspect of these maps is that their titles included the words "Puerto de San Francisco." For the first time the name San Francisco was associated with modern San Francisco Bay, and was omitted from the present Drakes Bay. Also of note is that Yerba Buena Island was named "Isla de Alcatraces" [Pelican Island], while modern Alcatraz Island was unnamed. (*See page 23.*)

There is one obvious error on the 1781 map. The stream marked with a lower-case **b** has the name "Rio de la Salud," a name applied by the Portolá expedition in 1769 to what is now Waddell Creek. But Waddell Creek is south of Año Nuevo Point, and the stream on the map is north of that point, where Whitehouse Creek is.

Log of the *San Carlos*

The first ship to enter San Francisco Bay

Under command of Lieutenant of Frigate of the Royal Navy Don Manuel de Ayala

Starting from the shelter of Monterey, situated at latitude 36° 33′, longitude 16° 45′ W. of San Blas to the newly-discovered Port of San Francisco, July 26, 1775.

That day it was impossible to sail on account of the wind coming from a contrary direction.

On July 27th, the launch towed the San Carlos until she came to the range of a southwest wind and sailed in a northwest direction. At noon Point Pinos was seen bearing south 13° distant five miles; at 3 p.m. it had disappeared from view. Very soon after, Point Año Nuevo and the land adjoining it came in sight, about four or five miles distant. From July 28th to August 3rd, little progress was made on account of contrary winds from the northwest. On August 3rd, at 1 p.m., land was seen to the east ¼ northeast, distant about twelve leagues. It was found to be Point Año Nuevo. At 7 p.m. another point came into view bearing north ¼ northeast, distant about twelve leagues, which was considered to be Point Reyes. At 10 p.m., the wind being northwest, the San Carlos steered west-southwest and continued in that course until 8 a.m. of the 4th, when the heading was changed to the north-northeast. At noon the sun's altitude was taken and the latitude was found to be 37° 11′, and longitude 17° 51′ W. of San Blas. At 6 p.m., August 4th, the southernmost Farallon of the Port of San Francisco was seen to the northwest, distant about eight leagues. The land to the north was Point Reyes, bearing 4° W., distant about fourteen leagues. At half past eleven, considering the coast was near, the course was changed to the south-southwest until 3 a.m. of August 5th, when it was changed again to the north-northeast 5° north to bring the ship at sunrise to the point it had been at sunset of the day before. At 5 a.m. four of the Farallones of San Francisco were seen to the north-northwest, distant four leagues. Point Año Nuevo was southeast ¼ east from twelve to fourteen leagues and Point Almejas northeast 4° east, distant three leagues. At 8 a.m., being near land, commander Ayala lowered the launch, and in it Pilot Cañizares was sent with ten men to search for an anchorage, while the San Carlos continued along the coast. At 9 a.m. a strong current was felt, which drove them to sea, but at eleven it was observed that the vessel was nearing the coast, which convinced the commander that it was due to the tide, and this was confirmed by the soundings; in entering the port, as on the first occasion, the tide was going out, and on the second one the tide was coming in.

The altitude of the sun was taken at noon of that day, with the utmost care, and the latitude was found to be 37° 42' and the longitude 17° 14' W. of San Blas. At this time Point Año Nuevo was about fourteen leagues distant to the southeast ¼ south; the Farallones to the northwest, distant four leagues, and Point Reyes north ¼ northeast, distant four leagues. The wind was from the west. At 4 p.m. the vessel was steered to the north-northeast, and half an hour later soundings were taken and bottom found at sixteen brazas[1] of mud and sand mixed, and distant from the mouth about two leagues. At 5 p.m. bottom was found at fifteen brazas, with the same kind of bottom material. Sounding was continued, and the bottom was found to be as noted in the large map. The current was so great at the mouth of this port that at 8:30 p.m., with a strong wind from the west-southwest with full sails, the current allowed them to go not more than a mile and a half per hour, which shows that the current must be at least six miles per hour at the middle of the channel. The swiftness of the current, the fact that the launch had not returned and that night was coming on, made it necessary to seek an anchorage. This was done with great care and precaution. Since the force of the wind made it necessary to have full sail, it was feared that some of the rigging might give way. For that reason, soundings were taken continually with a 20-lb. lead, and a line of sixty brazas could not reach bottom, either in the channel or near the point. This seemed very strange until it was realized that the current was carrying the lead, and it did not strike bottom. They continued thus until they were one league inside the mouth of the bay and a quarter of a mile from the shore, when the wind suddenly stopped. Finding that the current was carrying

---

1. Braza—approximately a fathom; 5.48 feet.

the ship back towards the mouth, an anchor was dropped, after having made it fast to the big mast so that if it did not catch the bottom it would not be lost. It was found that the anchor held. Two more anchors were made ready to drop in case the big one should drag. When the wind stopped and the current ceased, the vessel was found to be in twenty-two brazas, with sandy bottom.[2]

At 6 a.m. of August 6, the launch, which had not been seen since sunset the day before, came to the vessel. The pilot was asked why he had not come to meet the ship when he saw her sailing shoreward looking for the entrance of the bay, answered that at 6 p.m. he had seen a suitable harbor for the packet-boat to the east of the entrance, and when he attempted to go out, the whirlpools and eddies caused by the current were such that it was impossible to make any progress, as the current carried him back towards the shore, so that he determined to stay in the harbor he had attempted to leave. This, and the fact that the men were tired out, made him wait until 4 a.m., when he again attempted to go out, with the same result as before. During his efforts to get out, he saw the packet-boat, and putting the bow towards her he had no difficulty in reaching her.

At 7 a.m., the commander sent the pilot to examine a harbor that was to the west-northwest. He found it useless, because though it had sufficient water, the bottom was sticky mud. Since Ayala was not in need of shelter then, he did not enter that harbor, because he was afraid of losing his anchor in the mud, and also because it was open from the south to the east, although the wind came from the landward, which was about two leagues from the harbor.[3] He called this harbor "Carmelita," because in it was a rock resembling a friar of that order. There was in its vicinity an Indian village, the inhabitants of which came out from their huts and cried out and made signs for the vessel to go near them. While the sailors were taking soundings and came near the shore, the Indians erected a pole, at the top of which was a large number of feathers. The sailors having no orders to answer them, remained at a distance from the shore. The Indians, thinking, no doubt, that the sailors were afraid of them, endeavored to assure them by dropping their bows to the ground, and after describing a circle in the air with the arrows, stuck them in the sand. The launch came on board again, and soon after, the Indians, from a point of land near the vessel, talked to the sailors with loud cries, and although their voices were

2. Ayala anchored inside Fort Point—at what later was called the Presidio anchorage.
3. Richardson Bay.

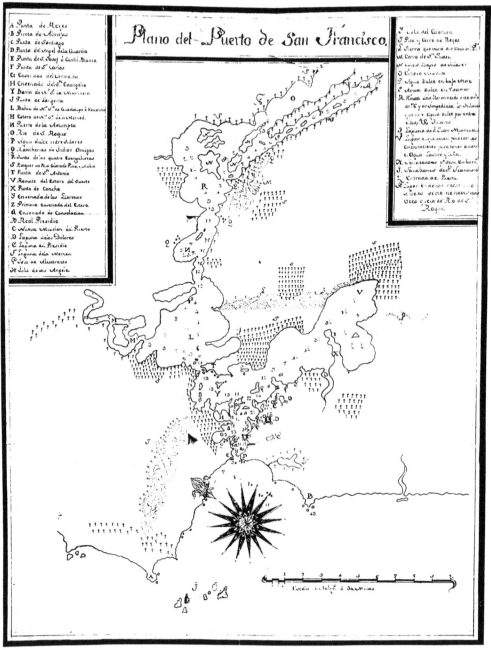

José de Cañizares: Plano del Puerto de San Francisco, 1776.

(Inscription from the 1781 map, opposite page.)

PLAN DEL GRAN PUERTO DE SAN Francisco descubierto y demarcado por el Alferez graduado de Fragata de la Real Armada, Dn. Jose de Cañizares primer Piloto del Departmento de San Blas, situado en la Costa Occidental de la California al Norte de la Linea, en el Mar Asiatico en Latitud Norte 37 gs. 44 minutos, y gravado por Manuel Villavicencio Añ. de 1781.

MAP OF THE GREAT PORT OF SAN Francisco, discovered and demarcated by the graduate Ensign of the Spanish Royal Navy, Don Jose de Cañizares, first Pilot of the District of San Blas, situated on the West Coast of California to the North of the Line, in the Asian Sea in North Latitude 37 deg. 44 minutes, and engraved by Manuel Villavicencio in the Yr. of 1781.

José de Cañizares Plano del Gran Puerto de San Francisco, 1781.
(The map's inscription and its English translation are in the box on the opposite page.)

A. Bodega Head	Y. Petaluma Creek	Q. Forested areas	Z. Point Lobos
B. Point Reyes	J. Southhampton Bay	R. Vicinity of	a. Año Nuevo Point
C. Point Bonita	K. Suisun Bay	Redwood City	b. Whitehouse Creek
D. Lime Point	L. Various low islands	S. Coyote Point	c. San Pedro Point
E. Richardson Bay	M. San Joaquin River	T. Mission Creek	d. The Farallones
F. Belvedere Cove	N. Sacramento River	V. Presidio	e. The Golden Gate
G. San Rafael Bay	O. Friendly Indians	X. Mission Dolores	f. Angel Island
H. San Pablo Bay	P. Oakland—not on map	I. Fort Point	g. Yerba Buena Island

heard distinctly, they could not be understood for want of an interpreter. At 9 the launch was sent again to another harbor to the north, which seemed to be better sheltered and to have better anchorage. It was so, and when the launch returned at 10, the pilot stated that he found bottom at eight to fourteen brazas, and the bottom was sticky with mud. At 3 p.m. the vessel sailed towards the place examined, but a strong current prevented her reaching it. It was then they decided to anchor in fifteen brazas, sandy bottom, and they stayed there all night, during which time the vessel moved on account of the bad quality of the anchors.

On the 7th, at 9 a.m., the vessel was started towards a large and fine-looking harbor, which seemed commodious. Soundings were taken, and the bottom was found at twelve to fourteen brazas. It had been decided to go to the end of it, but the tide was contrary and it was necessary to return to the vessel at 1 p.m. Indians from the shore were calling to the men with loud cries, and the commander decided to send the launch with the priest, the pilot, and armed men, with orders that they must not molest the Indians but treat them well and make them presents, for which purpose the commander gave the men beads and other trinkets and ordered them to observe good precaution, so that in case the Indians showed fight they could always easily return to the launch, where four armed men must always remain to protect the retreat. It is true that from the day when intercourse was first had with the Indians, it was seen how affable and hospitable they were, showing the greatest desire for the Spaniards to go to their village, where, they said, they could eat and sleep. They had already prepared on shore a meal of pinole, bread from their corn, and tamales of the same. During the time the Spaniards were with the Indians, they found that the latter repeated the Spanish words with great facility, and by signs the Spaniards asked the Indians to go on board the packet-boat, but the Indians, also by signs, signified that until the Spaniards should visit their village, they could not go on board. After a little while the Spaniards returned to the boat and the Indians disappeared.

On the 8th, the pilot, with men, was sent in the launch to explore the bay, and on the 9th returned and made his report.

On the 12th the launch was lowered to look for a better anchorage near Angel Island, which is the largest in this bay, and many good places were found. It was also thought a good idea to examine another island, which was found to be very steep and barren and would not afford shelter even for the launch. This island was called "Alcatraz"[4] on account of the abundance of those birds that were on it.

On the 13th the vessel moved to another anchorage with nine brazas of water at pistol shot of the land. On the 21st, the first pilot, Don José de

Cañizares, returned from an expedition on which he had been sent a few days before and made his report. On the same day, the second pilot, Don Juan B. Aguirre, went, with fresh men, in the launch to try to find the party which the commander of the presidio had promised to send to San Francisco by land. The second pilot did not see the party, but explored an estero that enters the land about twelve leagues.[5]

On the 23rd fifteen Indians came on a raft and were taken on board, where they were entertained and given something to eat. They learned how to ask for bread in Spanish.

From this day to the 6th of September, the explorations of the Bay of San Francisco continued, and first pilot Don José de Cañizares was instructed to make his report and the map of the bay.

On September 7th an attempt was made to go to sea for the return voyage, but the rudder was injured by a submerged rock on which the current had carried the vessel.

From this day to September 18th, the time was passed in repairing the rudder and making preparations for the return voyage, which took place on that day, going to Monterey, where they arrived the following day.

In order to make the necessary repairs to the ship and pass the equinox in good shelter, the San Carlos remained in the harbor of Monterey until October 13, 1775, when she started for San Blas, where she arrived on November 6th of the same year.

Reconnaissance of the Port of San Francico, with Map

Report of the Pilot Don José de Cañizares to
Commander Don Juan de Ayala

DEAR CAPTAIN:—During the four times that I made reconnaissance of this Port, and made its map, I found at the northeast and north-northeast what is shown on the map and I here describe.—To the north-northeast of Angel Island, distant about a mile, there is a bay running in a direction north-northwest to south-southwest. The distance between the points forming said bay is about two leagues, and the shore line is about two and a half leagues. To the northwest of the shore there are three small islands, forming between them and the shore a narrow passage of shallow water

---

4. Pelican. The name "Isla de Alcatraces" was applied originally to what is now Yerba Buena Island.

5. The southern portion of San Francisco Bay.

The *San Carlos* sails through the Golden Gate.
(From a painting by Walter Francis.)

closed to the southwest. The bay is all surrounded with hills with few trees, which are mostly laurel and oak, but at a distance to the west-north-west is visible a wood of what seems to be pines. In the middle of this bay is standing a high farallon with submerged rocks around it. On the north-east of it there is sufficient water for anchorage, as is shown on the map. There is no doubt of its being good anchorage for vessels, provided they have good cables and anchors, for they are subject to great stress because of the current, which at this point cannot be less than four miles an hour.[6]

North-northeast of said bay there is a mouth about two miles wide, where there are four small white rocks, the two north ones with the two south ones form a channel of nine brazas depth.[7]

From this, one passes to another bay[8] more spacious, the diameter of which is about eight leagues, its shape a perfect isosceles triangle; its mouth is divided into two channels—one, on the side of the southwest coast, turns to the northwest at about the distance of a mile and ends in two large harbors, which are situated in the same shore at about four league's distance from the mouth that communicates with the first bay. From the northwest point of the furthest harbor to the north of it, distant about one and a half leagues, in turning a point to the west-northwest, a large body of water is seen,[9] which I did not examine because the channel that leads to it is extremely limited, its depth not having three codos[10] of water. From here to the east-northeast follows a low-lying island, just above the water level, ending in a division made by the hills.[11] The other channel, which is roomy and deep, runs directly in a northeast direction till it reaches the division of the hills through a cañon that runs in the same direction.

All the bay, which is called the round bay (Bahia Redondo), though it is not shaped that way, is surrounded with steep hills, without trees, except-ing two spots on the slopes fronting the two harbors to the southwest. The rest of it is arid, rugged, and of a melancholic aspect. Outside of the channels there is in this bay about five codos of water, and at low tide two and a half, and in some places it is dry. It is not difficult to enter this bay, but going out will be difficult on account of the wind from the southwest.

---

6. This is the body of water between Point San Pedro, Point San Pablo, Point Richmond, and the Tiburon Peninsula. The high farallon is Red Rock.
7. The rocks are The Sisters and The Brothers.
8. San Pablo Bay.
9. Napa Slough
10. Codo—1.5 feet.
11. Mare Island. The division of the hills, or cañon, is Carquinez Strait.

After a careful examination of its shore, I did not find any fresh water or any signs of it. Standing in the cañon, which is to the northeast, there is a channel a mile and a half wide, deep and clear.[12] East of its entrance there is a ranchería of about four hundred souls. I had dealings with them, but did not buy anything, though I presented them with beads, which you had given me for that purpose, and some old clothing of mine. Their acquaintance was useful to my men and to me, as they presented us with exquisite fishes (amongst them salmon), seeds, and pinole. I had opportunity of visiting them four times and found them always as friendly as the first time, noticing in them polite manners, and what is better, modesty and retirement in the women. They are not disposed to beg, but accept with good will what is given them, without being impertinent, as are many others I have seen during the conquest. This Indian village has some scows or canoes, made of tule, so well constructed and woven that they caused me great admiration. Four men get in them to go fishing, pushing with two-ended oars with such speed that I found they went faster than the launch. These were the only Indians with whom I had communication in this northern part.

Following said channel a distance from its mouth, there is a harbor, so commodious, accessible, abundant in fresh water and wood, and sheltered from all winds, that I considered it one of the best inland ports that our Sovereign has for anchoring a fleet of vessels. I called it Puerto de la Asumpta, having examined it the day of the festivity of that saint.[13]

To the southeast of this port the cañon continues, until it joins the channel of the Indian village. Following a distance of three leagues in an east-northeast direction, it enters another bay[14] with a depth of thirteen brazas, diminishing to four where some rivers[15] empty and take the saltiness of the water which there becomes sweet, the same as in a lake. The rivers come, one from the east-northeast (this is the larger, about two hundred and fifty yards wide), the other, which has many branches, comes from the northeast through tulares and swamps in very low land, the channels not over two brazas with sandy bars at their mouths, where I found in sounding the water not more than a half braza. This made me think they were not navigable, especially as on the second occasion I entered them, I touched bottom both in the channels and on the bars. The

---

12. Carquinez Strait.
13. The Assumtion of the Virgin, August 15. Now named Southhampton Bay.
14. Suisun Bay.
15. The Sacramento and the San Joaquin.

bay where these rivers empty is another port larger than the Asumpta, where any vessel may enter, but it would be difficult to obtain wood, which is far from the shore. All the eastern coast is covered with trees; that to the west is arid, dry, full of grasshoppers, and impossible of settlement. This is all I have reconnoitered to the north of Angel Island. To the southeast of said island following the estero is as follows:

To the east of this island, at a distance of about two leagues, there is another, steep and barren, without any shelter, which divides the mouth of the channel in two,[16] through which the sea enters to a distance of about twelve leagues. The width of this channel is in some parts, one, two, and three leagues; its depth is not over four brazas, its width ample, but a pistol shot outside of the channel; its depth is not over two brazas. The extreme end of this sound, eastward, forms with a point, a pocket, which at low tide is nearly dry.[17] In every part there are seen poles driven in [the mud], with black feathers, bunches of tule, and little shells, which I believe are buoys for fishing, since they are in the water. I think it will be impossible to anchor for three leagues inside of this slough, because it is so exposed to the weather that strong cables and good anchorage are needed to hold against the strong current from the north.

The northeast part of this slough is surrounded by high hills, and has in its mouth a thick wood of oaks, and at the other end groves of thick redwood trees. At the southwest of the coast is a small slough, navigable only by launches,[18] and on the coast two harbors[19] where vessels can anchor. On the more eastern one there is an Indian village, rough, like the ones in Monterey. This part seems to have better places for missions, though I did not examine it except from a distance.

. . . I sign [this report] in this new Port of San Francisco, at the shelter of Angel Island, on September 7th, 1775.

José de Cañizares

---

16. Yerba Buena Island.
17. The Oakland and Berkeley tidal flats.
18. Islais Creek.
19. Yerba Buena Cove and Mission Bay.

The mission and presidio in what is now San Francisco were founded in 1776 by an expedition of settlers and soldiers led by Juan Bautista de Anza. Anza and two padres, Francisco Garcés and Pedro Font, kept diaries on the expedition, and are the authorities concerning the chronology of events and the description of the details of travel, of the landscape, and of the Indians. The party departed from Sonora, Mexico on September 29, 1775, and Font and others returned there on June 1, 1776.

The excerpts in this chapter are from the so-called "Short Diary" of Fray Pedro Font, which was first published in English in 1913, by the Academy of Pacific Coast History. Font (d. 1781) was not only a diarist; he was also something of a navigator, geographer, artist, and cartographer, as will be seen on the following pages.

Diary of Pedro Font

The Anza Expedition of 1775–1776

March 23, 1776.—We set out from the presidio of Monterey at half-past nine in the morning with the lieutenant and eleven soldiers and, at a quarter to four, halted on the other side of the Valle de Santa Delfina at the entrance of a canyon in the place called La Natividad, having traveled some eight long leagues: rather more than one league to the east; three, to the northeast with some deviation to the north, to where we crossed the Río de Monterey; then, about three to the northeast and one to the north-northeast.[1] [See the map on the next page.]

March 24.—We set out from La Natividad[2] at a quarter to eight in the morning and, at a quarter past four in the afternoon, halted at the Arroyo de las Llagas,[3] having traveled some twelve leagues: two to the northeast, and a little to the east when we ascended the mountain to go down to the Arroyo de San Benito;[4] one, north; two, northeast with some deviation to the north, to where we crossed the Río del Páxaro;[5] one almost due north; three, north-northwest through the Valle de San Bernardino;[6] and three, to the northwest.

March 25.—We set out from the Arroyo de las Llagas at a quarter to

---

1. Río de Monterey and Valle de Sta. Delfina are the Salinas River and its valley.
2. There is still a community named Natividad, about five miles northeast of Salinas.
3. On November 25, 1774, Padre Francisco Palou named a place near this creek *Las Llagas de Nuestro Padre San Francisco*—the Wounds, or Stigmata, of Our Father Saint Francis. Still named Llagas Creek, a tributary of the Pajaro River.
4. San Benito Valley—"Valle de Sn. Pasqual" on the map.
5. The Pajaro River, which still has the same name, was named on October 6, 1769 by the Portolá expedition.
6. Gilroy Valley.

**Font's "Plan or Map of the Journey that we made from Monterey
to the Port of San Francisco."**

The map shows the routes of the explorers in 1776. Font drew this map at the mission at
Tubutama, Mexico in 1777 after he had returned from California. The schooner *Sonora*, at
the upper left, refers to the discovery of Bodega Bay by Juan Francisco Bodega y Cuadro
in October 1775. The map also shows the route of the later explorations of March and
April 1776. Note "Sierra Nevada" at the upper right. On April 2, Font wrote (from a
hilltop east of present-day Antioch): "Looking to the northeast . . . about forty leagues off,
we saw a great snow-covered mountain range" (*una gran sierra nevada*)—the origin of the
name.

eight in the morning and, at four in the afternoon, halted at the Arroyo de San Joseph Cupertino,[7] having traveled some twelve leagues: three to the northwest; two northwest by west; five, west-northwest; and two, west by north.

March 26.—We set out from the Arroyo de San Joseph Cupertino at half-past seven in the morning, and, at a quarter to four in the afternoon, halted at a small, almost dry watercourse, about one short league after crossing the Arroyo de San Mateo, having traveled some twelve leagues: one, northwest; then some four west-northwest, to where we crossed the Arroyo de San Francisco; then, three northwest by west; and three, west-northwest.

March 27.—We set out from the small watercourse at seven in the morning and, a little after eleven, halted beside a pond or spring of fine water[8] near the mouth of the port of San Francisco, having traveled some six leagues; the first three to the northwest, and the last three, north-north-west and even very nearly north.

The port of San Francisco—marked on the map with the letter H—is a wonder of nature, and may be called the port of ports, on account of its great capacity and the various bights included in its littoral or shore and in its islands. The mouth of the port, which appears to be very easy of access and safe, may be about one league in length, and rather more than a league in width on the outside looking to the sea, and about a quarter of a league on the inside looking toward the port. The inner end of the entrance is formed by two very steep and high cliffs, on this side a white cliff, and on the other side a red one, and they face directly south and north. The outer end of the entrance is formed on the other side by some great rocks,[9] and on this side by a high and sandy hill which almost ends in a round point and has at its skirt in the water some white rocks like little farallones; this point Commander Rivera reached when he came to explore this port, and planted a cross upon it.[10]

The coast of the entrance on the other side runs from east-northeast to west-southwest; this I observed on the first of April, from the other side of the estuary or port, when I went there, and it appears to be all of red rocky material. The coast of the entrance on this side runs from northeast to southwest, not straight but forming a bend, on the beach of which a stream

---

7. Stevens Creek.
8. Mountain Lake.
9. Point Bonita.
10. Point Lobos.

empties that flows from the pond where we halted; we called it the Arroyo del Puerto.[11] The boat can reach this stream to get water, for on the entire stretch of the shore at the mouth the sea is quiet and the waves do not break on the beach as they do on the shore of the open sea. The Punta de Almejas,[12] in relation to the outer point of the entrance on this side, lies to the south, and must be some three leagues distant in an air-line. The beach, which consists of sand-dunes, forms almost a semicircle. The Punta de Reyes, on the other side, in relation to the said outer point of the entrance, lies northwest by west; the coast, as far as the said point, must be some twelve leagues in length, and does not run evenly, but forms a bight or bay, which is not very large, from what I could see at a distance of about three or four leagues. Some six or eight leagues out to sea, a group of rather large rocky islets (*farallones*) can be seen—they have this form: [see Figure 1, line 4] and lie, in relation to the outer point of the entrance, west by south. West of the said point, farther out, four other farallones can be seen—they look like this: [see Figure 1, line 8].

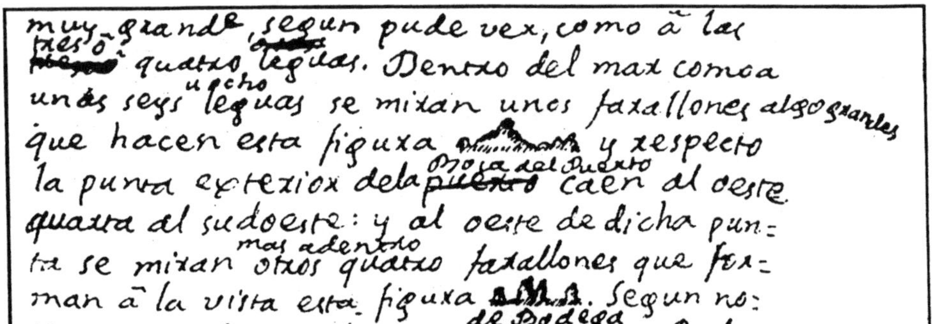
muy grande, segun pude ver, como a las
tres ó quatro leguas. Dentro del mar como a
unas seys u ocho leguas se miran unos farallones algo grandes
que hacen esta figura y respecto
la punta exterior dela Boca del Puerto caen al oeste
quarta al sudoeste: y al oeste de dicha punta se miran mas adentro otros quatro farallones que forman a la vista esta figura. Segun no-
ticias que adquiri, el puerto de Bodega por el sr capitan de la Goleta Dn Juan de la
descubierto dia 3. de Octubre de 1775, cae Quadra
unas quatro leguas al norte de la punta de reyes, situa y Bodega
do bajo la latitud de 38° 18'
cuya boca la forman la punta del cordon

Figure 1.

From the interior point of the entrance runs the wonderful port of San Francisco; this consists of a great bay or *estero*, as they call it, which must be some twenty-five leagues in length, and, as seen from the entrance, runs about southeast and northwest; at the middle is the entrance or mouth. The greater part of the shore of the port, as I saw it when we made the circuit

11. Lobos Creek.
12. San Pedro Point.

of it, is not clear, but miry, marshy, and full of ditches, and is consequently bad. The width of the port is not uniform—at the southeastern end it must be a league; in the middle, some four leagues; and at the northwestern end it terminates in a great bay of upwards of eight leagues, as it seemed to me. I found the shore of this bay clean, and not marshy like the former; in shape it is nearly round, although various bights were noticed in it, which at so great a distance prevented me from clearly distinguishing its shape. At about the middle of the bay, along the coast of this side, is the outlet or mouth of what has hitherto been taken to be a very large river, and has been called the Rio de San Francisco; I shall, henceforth, call it the Boca del Puerto Dulce,[13] because of the investigations that were made when we went to examine it, of which I shall speak later.

Inside the port I counted eight islands, and I cannot state whether there are more. The first to be met upon entering the port . . . is called the Isla de Angel, or de los Angeles; behind it the *San Carlos* anchored. It must be one short league in length and, seen from the entrance, has this form: [see Figure 2.] Opposite the entrance there is a very small islet, like a farallon, and another, not so small; and about southeast, another large one. Another quite long one can be seen at the southeastern end, very close to land. Another, about three leagues in length, also close to the land, is seen towards the northwest from the entrance; near it there are two other small ones, which, apparently, begin on that side to form the great bay in which terminates all this immense body of water; this being closed in and surrounded by mountains is as quiet as in a cup. Finally, in the bay and

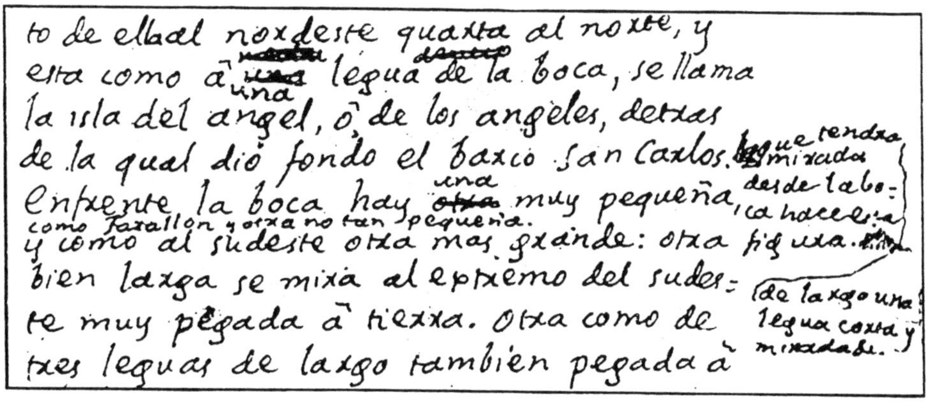

Figure 2.

---

13. "Mouth of the Sweetwater Port"—Carquinez Strait.

opposite the Boca del Puerto Dulce, there is a medium-sized island, besides those already mentioned.

March 28.—The commander decided to erect the holy cross on the extremity of the white cliff at the inner point of the entrance to the port, and we went there at eight o'clock in the morning. We ascended a small low hill, and then entered a table-land (*mesa*), entirely clear, of considerable extent, and flat, with a slight slope towards the port; it must be about half a league in width and a little more in length, and keeps narrowing until it ends in the white cliff.[14] This mesa commands a most wonderful view, since from it a great part of the port is visible, with its islands, the entrance, and the ocean, as far as the eye can reach—even farther than the farallones. The commander marked this mesa as the site of the new settlement, and the fort which is to be established at this port, for, from its being on a height it is so commanding that the entrance of the mouth of the port can be defended by musket-fire, and at the distance of a musket-shot there is water for the use of the people, that is, the spring or pond where we halted.

I again examined the mouth of the port and its configuration with a graphometer, and attempted to survey it; the plan of it is the one I here set down. [See the **Plan de la Boca del Puerto de San Francisco,** opposite.]

les miradas desde el arroyo de San matheo hacen esta figura .... *para ver si en aquellas imediaciones hallaba buenas propor-ciones para la comodidad de la nueba po-*

Figure 3.

From there the commander decided to go and inspect the low hills leading toward the inner part of the port—which, seen from the Arroyo de San Mateo have this form: [see Figure 3.] to see whether in those surroundings there were adequate facilities for the comfort of the new settlement. I accompanied the commander for a while, and, at ten in the morning, the commander and the lieutenant continuing the exploration, returned to the camp to make an observation. I observed the latitude of this port and found it to be 37° 49';[15] so I say: At the mouth of the port of San Francisco, March 28, 1776, meridian altitude of the lower limb of the sun, 55° 21'.

---

14. Fort Point.

15. The correct latitude, achieved by modern methods, is 37° 48' 38". Font's figure is an astonishingly accurate result considering his primitive instruments.

MAR DEL SUR.

Punta de Almejas.

¼ ½ 1 2
Escala de dos leguas Mexicanas.

Pedro Font's Map of the Entrance to San Francisco Bay, March 1776.

The top of the map is East. Font made this sketch from atop the cliff at Fort Point, which accounts for the northwest-southeast elongation. The drawing of a ship at the southeastern tip of Angel Island indicates the anchorage of the *San Carlos* in 1775. The route of the expedition is shown. The cross on the outer point (Point Lobos) marks the cross erected by Rivera in 1774, and the one at Fort Point was placed there by Anza and Font in 1776.

About five in the afternoon the commander and the lieutenant returned from their exploration very much pleased, as they had found more than they hoped for in the district of the low hills, which extended for some three leagues. In these hills and their canyons they found much brush and firewood, plenty of water in various springs or ponds, much tillable ground, and also plenty of pasture everywhere, so that the new settlement can obtain much wood, water, and grass or pasturage for their horses, all close at hand—there is lacking only timber for large edifices, although for huts and barracks, and for the stockade of the presidio there is sufficient material in the woods. With a little forethought, however, they can obtain the lumber just as they want it, for from about six leagues beyond the Arroyo de San Joseph Cupertino to some three leagues this side of the Arroyo de San Francisco there lies a plain about fifteen leagues in extent, called the Llano de los Robles[16] because it is very densely grown with all sizes of oaks, from which very good lumber may be taken out. Besides this, from the neighborhood of the Arroyo de las Llagas there extends as far as the Punta de Almejas a very high range, the greater part of it densely covered with spruce and other trees which extend as far as the Cañada de San Andrés, of which I shall speak tomorrow. From these places wood can be obtained in any desired quantity and size without much trouble, for it is not hard to get out.

The Indians that we saw on the road to Monterey seem to be gentle, good-natured, and very poor, and as they presented themselves unarmed they gave no sign of being warlike or ill-intentioned. Those who live near the port are pretty well bearded, but in color are not distinct from the others.

March 29.—At a quarter past seven in the morning we set out from the lake or spring where the Arroyo del Puerto has its source, and halted, at half-past six in the evening, at the Arroyo de San Mateo, having traveled some fifteen leagues by the roundabout which we took and of which I am going to speak, as from the port to the Arroyo de San Mateo it is only some six full leagues by the direct road.

As a result of the reconnaissance made yesterday, the commander decided to set out from the port by skirting the hills which surround it in the vicinity of the mouth, and to follow the inner shore until he should reach the level ground. For this reason he sent off the pack-train by the direct road with orders to stop at the Arroyo de San Mateo. We ourselves, taking

---

16. "Oak Plain"—Santa Clara Valley.

a different route, traveled about one league to the east, one to the east-southeast, and one to the southeast, and arrived at a beautiful stream, which, because this was the Friday of Sorrows, we called the Arroyo de los Dolores.

From a slight eminence, I here observed the lay of the port from this point and saw that its extremity lay to the east-southeast. I also noticed that a very high spruce tree, which is to be seen at a great distance, rising up, like a great tower, from the Llano de los Robles—it stands on the banks of the Arroyo de San Francisco; later on I measured its height.

March 30.—We set out from the Arroyo de San Mateo at a quarter past seven in the morning. . . . On setting out we followed, for some six leagues, the road we had come, taking the corresponding directions, until we arrived at the Arroyo de San Francisco. Beside this stream is the redwood tree I spoke of yesterday; I measured its height with the graphometer which they lent me at the mission of San Carlos del Carmelo, and, according to my reckoning, found it to be some fifty yards high, more or less; the trunk was five yards and a half in circumference at the base, and the soldiers said that there were still larger ones in the mountains.

For the purpose of going to examine the large river called the Río de San Francisco [the San Joaquin], which is said to flow into the port on the northern side, we here left the road by which we had come, and, changing our direction, followed the water. . . . We proceeded for some three leagues to the east; then, beginning to round the extremity of the port, we traveled about three leagues to the northeast. . . .

March 31.—We set out from the Río de Guadalupe at eight in the morning, and at four in the afternoon halted on the bank of the Arroyo de San Salvador—otherwise called the Arroyo de la Harina—having traveled some ten long leagues with varying directions . . . winding about until we got clear of the sloughs and low ground where we were, and gained higher ground along the foot of the hills that extend to the bay and the mouth of the Puerto Dulce. We then traveled, at a long distance from the water, for about two leagues to the north-northwest, and two more to the northwest.

April 1.—We set out from the Arroyo de la Harina at seven in the morning, and at half-past four in the afternoon halted at a small stream that had very little water, near the bay and about a league before you come to the Boca del Puerto Dulce. . . .

Just before arriving at the camp we looked out on the bay from a high hill, since from there most of it is visible, and I saw that it is surrounded on all sides by hills and mountains, except for a great opening that lies about west by north, in which direction a low tongue of land extends for a long stretch.

[The following is from *Font's Complete Diary*, edited by Herbert Eugene Bolton and published in 1931 by the University of California Press. The passage duplicates the information in the previous paragraph about ascending a hill, in the vicinity of where Mills College now is, whence the following sketch map was made.]

Then a little further on we ascended a hill which is in a straight line with the mainland and the plain which runs toward a very thick grove of oaks and live oaks on the banks of the estuary, and is almost made into an island by two arms of the estuary. From there I mapped this grove and the two arms of the estuary, and I am inserting the map here on the back of this sheet.

Font's sketch map of the East Bay shore, drawn on April 1, 1776.

The ESTERO is San Francisco Bay, still being treated as a branch of a greater entity. The two Brazos (arms) are San Leandro and San Antonio creeks—the same arms, seen from the opposite direction, that were on Crespí's 1772 map. The "Forest that is east-southeast of the Mouth of the Port" is the Alameda Peninsula and the future site of Oakland. The islands are Yerba Buena, Alcatraz, Angel, and Brooks. And at the upper right is the Boca (Mouth)—the Golden Gate.

Plano del Puerto de Sn. Francisco

Situado en la Costa Septentrional de California, por la Latitud de 37 grs. 54 mins. y en Longitud de 17 grs. 10 minuts. al Oeste del Puerto de San Blas, ò en 105 grs. 24 minuts. al Oeste de Thenerife; Lebantado ultimamente por los Pilotos de esta Carrera. Delineado por Dn. Josef Camacho Piloto Primero, del numero de la Rl. Arma. año 1779. Los numeros de sonda son brasas.

Map of the Port of San Francisco

Located on the Northern Coast of California, in Latitude 37 deg. 54 min. and Longitude 17 deg. 10 min. West of the Port of San Blas, or at 105 deg. West of Tenerife; recently mapped by the Pilots of this Service. Drawn by Don Josef Camacho, First Pilot, a member of the Royal Service, in the year 1779. The sounding numbers are in brasas [fathoms].

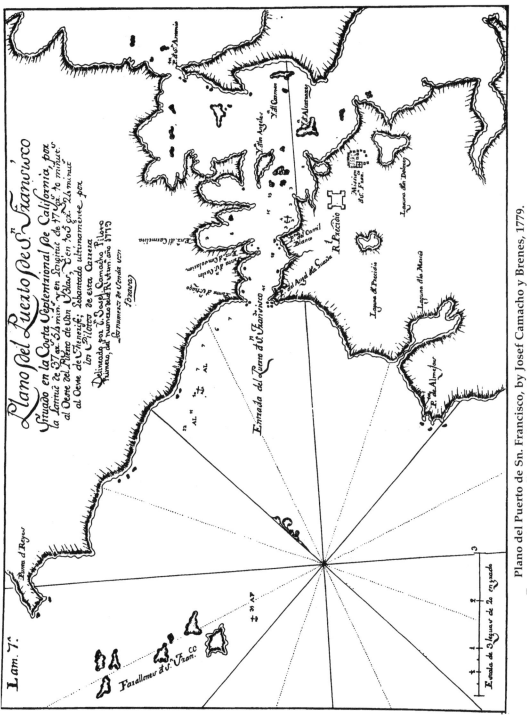

Plano del Puerto de Sn. Francisco, by Josef Camacho y Brenes, 1779.
Encompassing a smaller area than the Cañizares maps, but on a larger scale.
The surveying for this chart was accomplished in September and October 1779
by members of the Arteaga expedition, which was returning from Alaska.

The inscription on this map and its English
translation are in the box on the opposite page.

George Vancouver (1757–1798) entered the British Navy at age thirteen, and served under Captain James Cook on Cook's second (1772–74) and third (1776–80) voyages of discovery. He later was in the West Indies, and then was selected to command an expedition to the northwest coast of North America. In the course of his voyage he surveyed the coast from 56° N. down to 35° N., and entered San Francisco Bay.

He was an astute and perceptive observer, an excellent writer, and a pointed critic of conditions in "New Albion," as he referred to California, and of who was doing what to whom. The English and most Europeans had a low opinion of the Spanish—and it shows in Vancouver's comments and descriptions.

Vancouver made no effort to explore San Francisco Bay or its surroundings or to map or describe them. He apparently had with him the Dalrymple chart of the bay, (*see page 49.*) The only chart Vancouver himself created that is relevant to this book is of the entrance to San Francisco Bay, (*see page 45.*)

Captain George Vancouver
in command of the first non-Spanish
ship to enter San Francisco Bay

From:
*A Voyage of Discovery to the North Pacific Ocean
and Round the World*

Wₑ had approached, by two in the afternoon [of Wednesday, Nov. 14], within a small distance of the entrance into port St. Francisco, and found a rapid tide setting against us; the depth of water regularly decreased from 18 to 4 fathoms, which appearing to be the continuation of a shoal that stretches from the northern shore, then distant from us not more than a league, I hauled to the S. W. in order to avoid it, but did not succeed in reaching deeper water, as the bank we were upon extended a long way in that direction, as was evident from the confused breaking sea upon it, and the smooth water on either side of it. We therefore made for the port, and soon increased the depth of water to eight and ten fathoms, until we arrived between the two outer points of entrance, which are about two miles and a half apart, and bear from each other N. 10 W. and S. 10 E.; here we had 15 and 18 fathoms water, and soon afterwards we could gain no sounding with a hand-line.

Although favored with a pleasant breeze which impelled us at the rate of four or five knots an hour, it availed us no more than just to preserve our station against the ebb setting out of the port. We did not advance until four o'clock, and then but slowly, through the channel leading into this spacious port; lying in a direction N. 61 E. and S. 61 W.; it is nearly a league in length, with some rocks and breakers lying at a little distance from either shore. Those on the southern side were furthest, detached, and most conspicuous, especially one, about a mile within the S. W. point of entrance, which seemed to admit of a passage within it; but we had no opportunity of ascertaining that fact, nor is it of any importance to the navigation, as the main channel appeared to be free from any obstruction, and is of sufficient width for the largest vessels to turn in. Its northern shore, composed of high steep rocky cliffs, from the base of which a tract of sandy country commences, extending not only along the southern shore of the channel, and some distance along the exterior coast to the south-ward, but likewise to a considerable height on the more elevated land that borders thereon; and interspersed with huge massy rocks of different sizes, which, from the Farellones, render this point too conspicuous to be mis-taken. Having passed the inner points of entrance, we found ourselves in a very spacious sound, which had the appearance of containing a variety of as excellent harbours as the known world affords. The Spanish estab-lishment being on the southern side of the port, our course was directed along that shore, with regular soundings from nine to thirteen fathoms. Several persons were now seen on foot and on horseback coming to the S. E. point above mentioned; from whence two guns were fired, and an-swered by us, agreeably to the signal established between Senor Quadra and myself. As the night soon closed in, a fire was made on the beach, and other guns were fired; but as we did not understand their meaning, and as the soundings continued regular, we steered up the port, under an easy sail, in constant expectation of seeing the lights of the town, off which I purposed to anchor; but as these were not discoverable at eight at night, and being then in a snug cove, intirely land-locked, with six fathoms water and a clear bottom, we anchored to wait the return of day.

THURSDAY morning, Nov. 15th, we discovered our anchorage to be in a most excellent small bay [Yerba Buena Cove], within three fourths of a mile of the nearest shore, bearing by compass south; one point of the bay bearing N. 56 W., the other S. 73 E. the former at the distance of 2½, the latter about 3 miles. The herds of cattle and flocks of sheep grazing on the surrounding hills were a sight we had long been strangers to, and brought to our minds many pleasing reflections. These indicated that the residence of their proprietors could not be far remote, though we could perceive neither habitations nor inhabitants. On hoisting the colours at sun-rise, a gun was fired, and in a little time afterwards several people were seen on horseback coming from behind the hills down to the beach, who waved their hats, and made other signals for a boat, which was immediately sent to the shore, and on its return I was favored with the good company of a priest of the order of St. Francisco, and a sergeant in the Spanish army to breakfast. . . .

We attended them on shore after breakfast, where they embraced the earliest opportunity of proving, that their friendly expressions were not empty professions, by presenting me with a very fine ox, a sheep, and

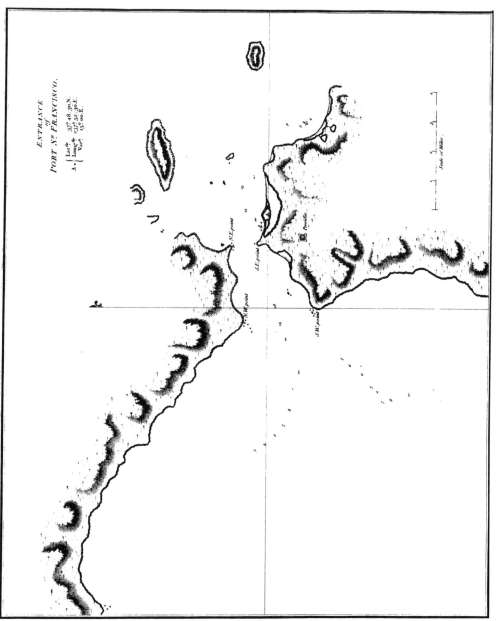

Entrance of Port of Sn. Francisco, by George Vancouver, 1792.

The chart shows Vancouver's routes of approach to and departure from the Golden Gate, with the depths given in fathoms. Angel and Yerba Buena islands are shown, but the only named feature is the Presidio. The official anchorage and Vancouver's anchorage in Yerba Buena Cove are marked by anchor symbols. Two ponds or lagoons are shown at the future site of Yerba Buena/San Francisco. These were at the foot of what later became Sacramento and Jackson streets.

some excellent vegetables. The good friar, after pointing out the most convenient spot for procuring wood and water . . . returned to the mission of St. Francisco, which we understood was at no great distance, and to which he gave us the most pressing invitation.

From these gentlemen we learned, that the station we had taken was far within the general anchoring place of the Spanish vessels, which they said was off that part of the shore where the light was shewn and guns fired the preceding night on the beach, near the entrance into the port. Our situation was however perfectly commodious and suitable to all our purposes, and with permission of the sergeant, I directed a tent to be pitched for the accommodation of the party employed in procuring wood and water; whilst the rest of the crew were engaged on board in repairing the damages sustained in our sails, rigging, &c. during the tempestuous weather with which we had lately contended.

From Senor Sal [an ensign in the Spanish army, and commandant of the port] I was made acquainted, that although the situation we had taken might answer our purposes in a certain degree, yet there was one which we had passed by the preceding evening, that we should find infinitely more commodious, as we should then be more immediately in his neighbourhood, and more frequent opportunities would be afforded him of rendering us service. In addition to the motive of his politeness, I was induced to comply with his wishes by the falling tide discovering to us a very great obstacle to our communication with that part of the shore from whence the wood and water were to be procured. A large bank of soft mud was found at low water to extend nearly half way between the ship and the shore.

In the afternoon a fresh breeze from the S. E. sprang up, attended with rainy disagreeable weather, which continued during the night; the next morning we had a strong gale from the S. and S. W. with heavy squalls and much rain. Having no time to spare, and the pilot sent by Senor Sal being arrived, we proceeded under double-reefed top-sails to the general place of anchorage, which we reached by noon, and took our station about a quarter of a mile from the shore in five fathoms water; the outer anchor was in 13 fathoms soft muddy bottom. In this situation the S. E. and N. W. points of the passage into this port, in a line, bore by compass S. 80 W. distant about half a mile. The flag staff at the Presidio bore S. 42 E.

The little we had seen of port St. Francisco enabled us to decide that it was very extensive in two directions; one spacious branch took its course east and southward to a great distance from the station we had quitted in the morning, the other apparently of equal magnitude led to the northward. In this were several islands.

Near the branch leading to the east and southeastward above mentioned, is situated the mission of Santa Clara. These gentlemen informed me, that this branch had been thoroughly examined, but that the branch leading to the north never had. . . .

The only Indian vessels we had met with, were without exception the most rude and sorry contrivances for embarkation I had ever beheld. The length of them was about ten feet, the breadth about three or four; they were constructed of rushes and dried grass of a long broad leaf, made up into rolls the length of the canoe, the thickest in the middle, and regularly tapering to a point at each end. These are so disposed, that on their ends being secured and lashed together the vessel is formed, which being broadest in the middle, and coming to a point at each extremity, goes with either end foremost. These rolls are laid and fastened so close to each other, that in calm weather and smooth water I believe them to be tolerably dry, but they appeared to be very ill calculated to contend with wind and waves. The wind now blew strong with heavy squalls from the S. W. and in the middle of the spacious inlet the sea broke with much force; notwithstanding which, as soon as these people had delivered their message, they crossed the inlet for the purpose of catching fish, without seeming to entertain the least apprehension for their safety. They conducted their canoe or vessel by long double-bladed paddles, like those used by the Esquimaux.

The S. W. wind attended by much rain, blew very hard until Saturday morning the 17th, when the weather becoming more moderate I visited the shore. I was greatly mortified to find, that neither wood nor water could be procured with such convenience, nor of so good a quality, as at the station we had quitted a league and a half within the entrance of the port on the southern shore; . . . A tent was immediately pitched on the shore, wells were dug for obtaining water, and a party was employed in procuring fuel from small bushy holly-leaved oaks, the only trees fit for our purpose. A lagoon of sea-water was between the beach and the spot on which these trees grew, which rendered the conveying the wood when cut a very laborious operation.

Whilst engaged in allotting to the people their different employments, some saddled horses arrived from the commandant with a very cordial invitation to his habitation; which was accepted by myself and some of the officers. We rode up to the Presidio, an appellation given to their military establishments in this country, and signifying a *safe-guard*. The residence of the friars is called a Mission. We soon arrived at the Presidio, which was not more than a mile from our landing place. Its wall, which fronted the harbour, was visible from the ships; but instead of the city or town, whose lights we had so anxiously looked for on the night of our arrival, we were conducted into a spacious verdant plain, surrounded by hills on every side, excepting that which fronted the port. The only object of human industry which presented itself, was a square area, whose sides were about two hundred yards in length, enclosed by a mud wall, and resembling a pound for cattle. Above this wall the thatched roofs of their low small houses just made their appearance. On entering the Presidio, we found one of its sides still uninclosed by the wall, and very indifferently fenced in by a few bushes here and there, fastened to stakes in the ground. The unfinished state of this part, afforded us an opportunity of seeing the strength of the wall, and the manner in which it was constructed. It is about fourteen feet high, and five feet in breadth, and was first formed by uprights and horizontal rafters of large timber, between which dried sods and moistened earth were pressed as close and as hard as possible; after which the whole was cased with the earth made into a sort of mud plaster, which gave it the appearance of durability, and of being sufficiently strong to protect them, with the assistance of their fire-arms, against all the force which the natives of the country might be able to collect.

The Spanish soldiers composing the garrison amounted, I understood, to thirty-five; who, with their wives, families, and a few Indian servants, composed the whole of the inhabitants. Their houses were along the wall, within the square, and their fronts uniformly extended the same distance into the area, which is a clear open space, without buildings or other interruptions. The only entrance into it, is by a large gateway; facing which, and against the centre of the opposite wall or side, is the church; which, though small, was neat in comparison to the rest of the buildings. This projects further into the square than the houses, and is distinguishable from the other edifices, by being white-washed with lime made from sea-shells; lime-stone or calcareous earth not having yet been discovered in the neighbourhood. On the left of the church, is the commandant's house, consisting, I believe, of two rooms and a closet only, which are divided by many walls, similar to that which encloses the square, and communicating with each other by very small doors. Between these apartments and the outward wall was an excellent poultry-house and yard, which seemed pretty well stocked; and between the roofs and ceilings of the rooms was a kind of lumber garret: these were all the conveniences the habitation seemed calculated to afford. The rest of the houses, though smaller, were fashioned exactly after the same manner; and in the winter, or rainy seasons, must at the best be very uncomfortable dwellings. For though the walls are a sufficient security against the inclemency of the weather, yet the windows, which are cut in the front wall, and look into the

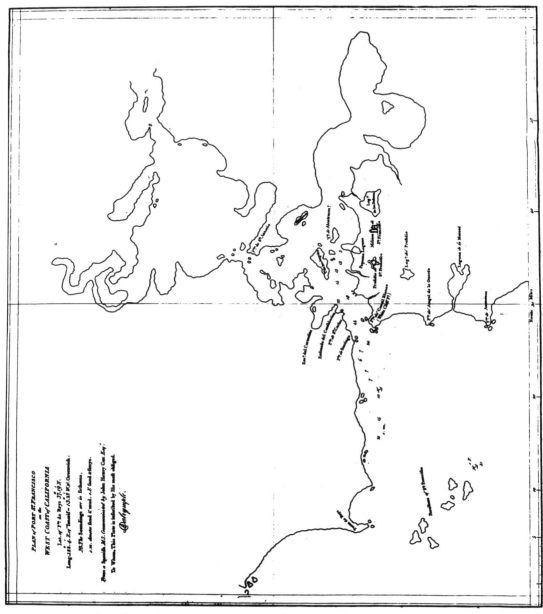

Plan of Port Sn. Francisco, published by Alexander Dalrymple in 1789.

PLAN of PORT Sⁿ· FRANCISCO on the WEST COAST of CALIFORNIA. Lat. of Pta. de Reys 37°.19′ N. Long. 122°.4′ E. of Tenerif – 13°.23′ W. fr. Greenwich. NB, The Soundings *are in* fathoms. *s.m. denotes* fand & mud. *s.F.* fand & fanyo. From a Spanish MS. Communicated by John Henry Cox Esq. To Whom, This Plate is infcribed by His moft obliged. Dalrymple.

The first chart of San Francisco Bay to be published in English. It is borrowed from Spanish sources, and in fact Dalrymple translated only one of the Spanish place names into English. A copy was said to have been in Vancouver's possession in 1792.

square, are destitute of glass, or any other defence that does not at the same time exclude the light.

The apartment in the commandant's house, into which we were ushered, was about thirty feet long, fourteen feet broad, and twelve feet high; and the other room, or chamber, I judged to be of the same dimensions, excepting in its length, which appeared to be somewhat less. The floor was of the native soil raised about three feet from its original level, without being boarded, paved, or even reduced to an even surface: the roof was covered in with flags and rushes, the walls on the inside had once been white-washed; the furniture consisted of a very sparing assortment of the most indispensible articles, of the rudest fashion, and of the meanest kind; and ill accorded with the ideas we had conceived of the sumptuous manner in which the Spaniards live on this side of the globe. . . .

Our excursion did not extend far from the Presidio, which is situated as before described in a plain surrounded by hills. This plain is by no means a dead flat, but of unequal surface; the soil is of a sandy nature, and was wholly under pasture, on which were grazing several flocks of sheep and herds of cattle; the sides of the surrounding hills, though but moderately elevated, seemed barren, or nearly so; and their summits were composed of naked uneven rocks. . . .

Thus, at the expence of very little examination, though not without much disappointment, was our curiosity satisfied concerning the Spanish town and settlement of St. Francisco. Instead of finding a country tolerably well inhabited and far advanced in cultivation, if we except its natural pastures, the flocks of sheep, and herds of cattle, there is not an object to indicate the most remote connection with any European, or other civilized nation. . . .

[The establishment] possesses no other means for its protection than such as have been already described; with a brass three-pounder mounted on a rotten carriage before the Presidio, and a similar piece of ordnance which (I was told) was at the S. E. point of entrance lashed to a log instead of a carriage; and was the gun whose report we heard the evening of our arrival. Before the Presidio there had formerly been two pieces of ordnance, but one of them had lately burst to pieces. . . .

The next day, Sunday the 18th, was appointed for my visiting the mission. Accompanied by Mr. Menzies and some of the officers, and our friendly Senor Sal, I rode thither to dinner. Its distance from the Presidio is about a league, in an easterly direction; our ride was rendered unpleasant by the soil being very loose and sandy, and by the road being much incommoded with low groveling bushes. . . .

The buildings of the mission formed two sides of a square only, and did not appear as if intended, at any future time, to form a perfect quadrangle like the Presidio. The architecture and materials, however, seemed nearly to correspond.

On our arrival, we were received by the reverend fathers with every demonstration of cordiality, friendship, and the most genuine hospitality. We were instantly conducted to their mansion, which was situated near, and communicated with the church. The houses formed a small oblong-square, the side of the church composed at one end, near which were the apartments allotted to the fathers. These were constructed nearly after the manner of those at the Presidio, but appeared to be more finished, better contrived, were larger, and much more cleanly. Along the walls of this interior square, were also many other apartments adapted to various purposes.

Whilst dinner was preparing, our attention was engaged in seeing the several houses within the square. Some we found appropriated to the reception of grain, of which, however, they had not a very abundant stock; nor was the place of its growth within sight of the mission; though the richness of the contiguous soil, seemed equal to all the purposes of husbandry. One large room was occupied by manufacturers of a coarse form of blanketting, made from the wool produced in the neighbourhood. . . .

The major part of [the Indians], I understood, were converted to the Roman Catholic persuasion; but I was astonished to observe how few advantages had attended their conversion.

. . . Deaf to the important lessons, and insensible of the promised advantages, they still remained in the most abject state of uncivilization; and if we except the inhabitants of Tierra del Fuego, and those of Van Dieman's land, they are certainly a race of the most miserable beings, possessing the faculty of human reason, I ever saw. Their persons, generally speaking, were under the middle size, and very ill made; their faces ugly, presenting a dull, heavy, and stupid countenance, devoid of sensibility or the least expression. One of their greatest aversions is cleanliness, both in their persons and habitations; which, after the fashion of their forefathers, were still without the most trivial improvement. Their houses were of a conical form, about six or seven feet in diameter at their base (which is the ground) and are constructed by a number of stakes, chiefly of the willow tribe, which are driven erect into the earth in a circular manner, the upper ends of which being small and pliable are brought nearly to join at the top, in the centre of the circle; and these being securely fastened, give the upper part or roof somewhat of a flattish appearance. Thinner twigs of the like species are horizontally interwoven between the uprights, forming a piece of basket work about ten or twelve feet high; at the top a small aperture is left, which allows the smoke of the fire made in the centre of the hut to escape, and admits most of the light they receive: the entrance is by a small hole close to the ground, through which with difficulty one person at a time can gain admittance. The whole is covered over with a thick thatch of dried grass and rushes.

These miserable habitations, each of which was allotted for the residence of a whole family, were erected with some degree of uniformity, about three or four feet asunder, in straight rows, leaving lanes or passages at right angles between them; but these were so abominably infested with every kind of filth and nastiness, as to be rendered not less offensive than degrading to the human species.

Close by stood the church, which for its magnitude, architecture, and internal decorations, did great credit to the constructors of it; and presented a striking contrast between the exertions of genius and such as bare necessity is capable of suggesting. The raising and decorating this edifice appeared to have greatly attracted the attention of the fathers; and the comforts they might have provided in their own humble habitations, seemed to have been totally sacrificed to the accomplishment of this favorite object. Even their garden, an object of such material importance, had not yet acquired any great degree of cultivation, though its soil was a rich black mould, and promised an ample return for any labour that might be bestowed upon it. The whole contained about four acres, was tolerably well fenced in, and produced some fig, peach, apple, and other fruit-trees, but afforded a very scanty supply of useful vegetables; the principal part lying waste and over-run with weeds. . . .

Amongst other things I understood, that this mission was established in the year 1775 [1776], and the Presidio of St. Francisco in 1778 [1776], and that they were the *northernmost settlements, of any description, formed by the court of Spain on the continental shore of North-West America, or the islands adjacent.* . . . The excursions of the Spanish seemed to be confined to the neighbourhood of their immediate place of residence, and the direct line of country between one station and another; as they have no vessels for embarkation excepting the native canoe, and an old rotten wooden one, which was lying near our landing place. Had they proper boats on this spacious sheet of water, their journies would not only be much facilitated, but it would afford a very agreeable variety in their manner of life, and help to pass away many of the solitary and wearisome hours which they must unavoidably experience.

I understood that the opposite of the port had been visited by some soldiers on horseback, who obtained but little information; some converted Indians were found living amongst the natives of the northern and western parts of the port, who were esteemed by the Spaniards to be a docile, and in general a well-disposed people; though little communication took place between them and the inhabitants of this side. The missionaries found no difficulty in subjecting these people to their authority. It is mild and charitable, teaches them the cultivation of the soil, and introduces amongst them such of the useful arts as are most essential to the comforts of human nature and social life. It is much to be wished, that these benevolent exertions may succeed, though there is every appearance that their progress will be very slow; yet they will probably lay a foundation, on which the posterity of the present race may secure to themselves the enjoyment of civil society.

. . . Our first place of anchorage [Yerba Buena Cove] possesses many advantages, superior to those we found at the second. The tides are there infinitely the most regular, and notwithstanding the bank of mud prevented our landing in some places, it does not extend all round the cove; for its south-western part is a steep shore, and might easily be made commodious for obtaining fuel and water; the latter is very good, and there is an abundance of the former immediately in its vicinity. The anchorage is more secure, by being completely land-locked, and further removed from the ocean.

Georg Heinrich von Langsdorff (1774–1852), a German-born scientist/physician, was with the Russian expedition commanded by Nikolai Petrovich Rezanov. Rezanov's major purposes in visiting San Francisco Bay were to acquire supplies to succor the population of the Russian base at New Archangel (modern Sitka, Alaska), which he had found in a starving condition, and to establish diplomatic relations with the Spanish.

Langsdorff visited the missions at San Francisco and San Jose, noted in great detail the lives and conditions of the Spanish and the Indians, and of the relationship prevailing between the two disparate groups. A man of many parts, he also was skilled at drawing; engravings made from his drawings appeared in his book *Observations of a Journey Around the World*, published in 1812.

Georg Heinrich von Langsdorff

From:
Narrative of the Rezanov Voyage to Nueva California in 1806.

Early in the morning [of March 27, 1806, Old Style] we saw, lying to the south, the group of rocks called Los Farallones del Puerto de San Francisco, and to the east the promontory of Punta de los Reyes, in latitude 37° 59′, near which lies the Puerto de San Francisco.

We were at this time carried by the current two miles to the south inside of an hour. Steering now directly for the puerto, we had much satisfaction in proving the correctness of Vancouver's charts and views, which left nothing further to be desired. His soundings will serve every navigator as a safe guide in running into the puerto even in the dark. We, however, deemed it more prudent to cast anchor, for the night, between two and three miles distant from the mouth of the puerto, in four and a half fathoms of water, and at daybreak of the 28th we headed for our destination. At about nine o'clock we reached the southeastern point of the puerto, on which, while yet at a considerable distance, we had perceived a fort. Upon approaching this fort we were challenged through a speaking-trumpet, and asked who we were and from whence we came. In consequence of our answer, we were ordered to cast anchor near the fort.

Hardly had we arrived at our destination on the morning of March 28, 1806, O.S., April 8, N.S., after a voyage of thirty-two days, when fifteen horsemen came out of the fort [El Fuerte de San Joaquin de] San Francisco, and advanced at full gallop to the shore near our place of anchorage. They demanded, by calls and signs, that we send a boat ashore, and manifested much impatience while we lowered one, and Lieutenant Davidov and myself went therein to the shore.

Here we were received by a Franciscan padre and several military officers, when a fine-looking young don, not otherwise distinguished from the others but by a singular garb, was presented to us as the comandante of the establishment. Over his uniform he wore a sort of mantle of striped woolen cloth, which resembled very much the coverlet of a bed, with a slit in the middle, through which his head passed, the longer part covering the breast and back, the narrower part the shoulders. He, as well as the other officers, wore peculiarly embroidered boots, of a particular make, with unusually large spurs. Most of them also had wide, full cloaks. As neither Lieutenant Davidov nor myself understood Spanish, the conversation was carried on in Latin, between me and the Franciscan padre, this being the only medium by which either one could make himself intelligible to the other.

The first inquiry made was as to who we were and whence we came. The reply was that our ship belonged to a Russian voyage of discovery, and that the commander thereof, His Excellency the Count Rezanov, was on board; that our intention had been to go to Monterey, as the seat of government, but that we were delayed by contrary winds, and that, owing to insufficiency of provisions, we had been under the necessity of putting into this port, as the nearest we could make. We therefore solicited the comandante's permission to purchase the needed supplies, and to make necessary repairs to our ship.

[Upon hearing the explanation offered by the Russians] they offered all necessary assistance, and entreated that Rezanov come ashore, saying they would remain and wait for him and conduct him to the residence of the comandante of the Presidio.

On our way to the Presidio we were told that the comandante permanente, Don José Darío Argüello, was absent, and that his son, the Alférez Don Luis Antonio, with whom we were then conversing, was comandante temporal until the return of his father. In a little more than a quarter of an hour we were at the Presidio, and here we were received in the most hospitable manner by Señora Argüello, esposa of the comandante permanente, and her family.

The whole establishment of [the Presidio de] San Francisco externally has the look of a German farmstead. Its low one-story buildings surround a somewhat long quadrangular court. The house of the comandante is small and mean. A whitewashed room, half of the floor of which was covered with straw matting, had but little furniture, and that of an inferior quality. The furnished half served as a reception-room. The welcome over, the refreshments were served, and we were invited to partake later of as good a dinner as their kitchen and larder would provide. It was not long before dinner was ready, and once again, after long privation, we enjoyed an excellent repast, and, to our great surprise, the poor quality of the house furniture considered, in a rich service of silver tableware. This precious

View of the Spanish establishments at San Francisco, 1806, by Wilhelm Gottlief Tilesius von Tilenau.
The first illustration of any part of the Bay Area. The scene depicts the buildings of the Presidio, as seen from the Golden Gate.

Mexican metal can be found in even the most remote Spanish possessions. Mutual esteem and harmony glowed without diminution in the conduct of this kindly family, who knew scarcely any other diversions or pleasures than those resulting from family joys and domestic happiness.

The Señora Argüello was the mother of fifteen children, and of these thirteen were living at this time. Some of the sons were absent upon military duty, and the others were at home. Of the grown-up unmarried daughters, the Doña Concepción most particularly interested us. She was distinguished for her vivacity and cheerfulness, her love-inspiring and brilliant eyes and exceedingly beautiful teeth, her expressive and pleasing features, shapeliness of figure, and for a thousand other charms, besides an artless natural demeanor. Beauties of her kind one may find, though but seldom, only in Italy, Portugal, and Spain.

We returned to the ship in the evening, much delighted with the day passed. On arriving we received the pleasing report that the comandante of the Presidio had sent far more supplies than our debilitated promyshleniki could consume in several days. Among the supplies were four large fat oxen, two sheep, onions and garlic, lettuce and cabbage, as well as several other kinds of vegetables.

At eight o'clock on the morning of the 29th the saddle-horses were waiting for us at the shore, as agreed upon, to carry us to the Misíon, and Padre Uría himself had come to conduct us. The Count Rezanov, Lieutenants Khvostov and Davidov, and myself, were in this pleasure-party. As we had to pass the Presidio on our way, we called there, just to bid good morning to the Argüello family, and were served with chocolate, after which we rode onward to the Misíon. The road thither is through loose sand, and is not good for either walking or riding. The surroundings are mostly bare, and the hills, covered in places with low shrubs, afford but little of anything interesting. Birds were almost the only things that attracted our attention, and I saw several kinds unknown to me. There were also a few rabbits and hares.

In the provincia of Nueva California, extending from San Francisco (latitude 37° 55′ N.), there are at the present time nineteen misiones, each of which has from six hundred to a thousand neófitos. Protection for the misiones is afforded by, if I am not mistaken, six presidios [correctly, four: San Francisco, Monterey, Santa Barbara, and San Diego], but, all told, there are not more than from two hundred to three hundred cavalry.

The Misíon Santa Clara de Asis, lying between San Francisco and Monterey, is, with regard to its fine situation, fertility of soil, population, and extent of buildings and grounds, considered the largest and richest misíon. All the misiones have cattle in great numbers, and an abundance of other productions necessary to the support of man, and the padres, in general, conduct themselves with such prudence, kindness, paternal care, and justice, in their attitude towards the neófitos, that tranquillity, happiness, obedience, and unanimity are the natural results of their methods. Corporal punishment commonly follows disobedience. The padres have recourse to the presidios only on very extraordinary occasions, as, for instance, when expeditions are sent out in pursuit of prospective converts, or when couriers carrying communications require protection, or as a precaution against sudden attacks.

There are seldom more than from three to five soldiers at any time at any misíon, but this seemingly small number has hitherto been always found sufficient to keep the Indians under proper restraint. I was assured by a person worthy of credit that the Spanish cortes does not spend less than a million piastres annually for the support of the misiones, and their military establishments, in the two Californias, and that, too, without deriving any advantage from them, other than the spreading of Christianity in these provincias of Nueva España.

Behind the residence of the frailes there is a large courtyard, inclosed by houses. Here live the Indian women of the Misíon, who are employed, under the immediate supervision of the padres, in useful occupations. such as cleaning and combing wool, spinning, weaving, etc. Their principal business is the manufacture of a woollen cloth and blankets for the Indians' own use. The wool of the sheep here is very fine, but the tools and looms are of a crude make. As the misioneros are the sole instructors of these people, who themselves know very little about such matters, scarcely even understanding the fulling, the cloth is far from the perfection that might be achieved.

All the girls and women are closely guarded in separate houses, as though under lock and key, and kept at work. They are but seldom permitted to go out in the day, and never at night. As soon, however, as a girl marries, she is free, and, with her husband, lives in one of the Indian villages belonging to the Misíon. These villages are called "las rancherías." Through such arrangements or precautions the misioneros hope to bind the neófitos to the misíon, and spread their faith with more ease and security. About a hundred paces from the buildings properly called the Misíon, lies one of these Indian villages or barracks. It consists of eight long rows of houses, where each family lives separate and apart from the others. The Indian neófitos here are about twelve hundred in number.

After satisfying our curiosity at the ranchería, we inspected several other serviceable institutions for the promotion of production and economy in the establishment. There was a building for melting tallow, and another for making soap; there were workshops for locksmiths and black-smiths, and for cabinet-makers and carpenters; there were houses for the storage of tallow, soap, butter, salt, wool, and ox-hides (these being articles of exportation), with storerooms for corn, pease, beans, and other kinds of pulse.

When one considers that in this way two or three misionero padres take upon themselves such a sort of voluntary exile from their country, only to spread Christianity, and to civilize a wild and uncultivated race of men, to teach them husbandry and various useful arts, cherishing and instructing them as if they were their own children, providing them with dwellings, food, and clothing, with everything else necessary for their subsistence, and maintaining the utmost order and regularity of conduct,—when all these particulars, I say, are considered, one cannot sufficiently admire the zeal and activity that carry them through labors so arduous, nor forbear to wish the most complete success to their undertaking.

Meanwhile we were called to dinner, and were served with a very appetizing soup seasoned with herbs of different kinds, roast fowl, leg of mutton, different kinds of vegetables dressed in different ways, salad, pastry, preserved fruits, and many sorts of food dishes prepared with milk. All these were things to which our palates had been so long strangers, that we were not a little pleased with them. The wine offered us had been brought from the peninsula of Antigua California, and was of but an ordinary quality. Soon after dinner we were served with tea of poor quality, and chocolate of super excellence.

Although we acquired but a slight knowledge of the Indians of this Misión on this day, yet I will combine here all that I learned concerning them with my observations during our entire stay.

The neófitos of the Misión San Francisco are the original inhabitants of these and the neighboring parts. A few come from the mouth of a large river that flows into the northernmost part of the harbor, and some from the neighborhood of Port Bodega, which lies to the north of San Francisco.

Their habitations are small round huts of straw, cone-shaped, erected at any stopping-place. These huts are burned upon their leaving, and the hut in which a person dies is also given to the flames. Both sexes go almost naked, wearing merely a girdle tied around the waist.

These Indians are of middling or rather short stature, and their color is of such a dark brown that it approaches black. This color is owing very much to their filthy mode of living, to the power of the sun's rays, to their custom of smearing their bodies with mud and ember-dust, and their slovenly way of wearing their scanty covering.

Their lips are large, thick, and protruding, their noses broad, flat, and negro-like. Their features in many respects resemble those of the negro, and their color also, but their black hair, however, is in the highest degree different, being long and straight. Left to grow naturally, it would often hang down even below the hips, but they commonly cut it to the length of four or five inches, when it sticks out like bristles, and this to the eyes of a European is very repellent. The forehead appears extremely low, as the hair grows very far down towards the eyes. The eyebrows are not very hirsute. The beard is but moderately thick, and many pinch out the hairs with mussel-shells.

None of the men that we saw were over five feet in height. They were badly proportioned, and their appearance was so dull, heavy, and neglectful, that we were all agreed that we had never before seen the human race on such a low level.

Tattooing is a common practice, but principally among the women. Some have a double or triple line from each corner of the mouth down to the chin, while others have, in the middle of the chin only, a few concentrical stripes, which converge. Many have simple long and cross stripes from the chin over the neck down to the breast, and upon the shoulders.

When it is considered that two or three padres and four or five soldiers keep in order a community of from a thousand to fifteen hundred rough and uncivilized men, and make them pursue a course of life wholly different from that to which they had always been accustomed, it must be presumed that the cause is principally to be found in the mildness and forbearance with which they are treated, and in the paternal care and kindness extended towards them. I must, however, also attribute the cause, in no small measure, to the simplicity of these poor creatures, who, in stature no less than in mind, are certainly of a very inferior race of human beings. I believe them wholly incapable of forming among themselves any regular and combined plan for their own emancipation.

But I will return to the religiosos of the misiones. Properly speaking, they are merely the stewards through whose instruction the neófitos obtain the comforts of life, a habitation, and food and clothing. The neófitos are principally employed in such work as husbandry, tending cattle, and shearing sheep, or in handiwork, such as building, preparing tallow, and making soap and household articles.

They are also employed in the transportation of provisions, as well as other goods, from one misíon or presidio to another. The most laborious work, the grinding of the corn, is left almost entirely to the women. It is rubbed between two quadrangular oblong stones until ground into meal. Although the flour made is very white, the bread is very heavy and hard.

The government has not, nor have the padres, anything in view other than the propagation of the Christian religion. Hence it may be supposed that the Indians, to whose maintenance and instruction all their efforts are devoted, must be much happier in their condition of comparative civilization than they were before, since they are permitted to retain their former habits and customs not interdicted by the misioneros.

In their dances, amusements, sports, ornaments, etc., they are liberally indulged. They have a little property of their own in fowls and pigeons. Upon obtaining permission, they may go hunting and fishing. Altogether, they can live much more free from care than in their previous wild, natural state.

Notwithstanding all that has been said in favor of the treatment of the Indians at the misiones, an irresistible desire for freedom sometimes breaks out in individuals. This may probably be referred to the natural genius of the race. Their attachment to a wandering life, their love of alternate diversion from hunting and fishing to entire idleness, seem, in their eyes, to overbalance all the benefits they enjoy at the misiones, and these to us appear very great. The result is, every now and then attempts to escape are made. On such occasions, no sooner is the neófito missed than search for him is at once begun, and as it is always known to what tribe he belongs, and on account of the enmity that subsists among the different tribes, he can never take refuge with any other,—a circumstance which perhaps he thought not of beforehand,—it is hardly possible for him to escape those sent in his pursuit. He is almost always brought back to the misión, where he is bastinadoed, and an iron rod a foot or a foot and a half long and an inch in diameter is fastened to one of his feet. This has a twofold use, in that it prevents the Indian from making another attempt to escape, and has the effect of terrifying the others and deterring them from indulging in escapades of a similar nature.

Sufficient attention is not paid to the conservation of health in Nueva California. The military alone have a physician and a surgeon, who live at the Presidio de Monterey. Neither the misioneros nor their adopted children, the Indians, are provided for medically. Although the climate is better and more salubrious here than in Antigua California, yet the Indians of the misiones are often attacked with fevers, and, being of weak constitutions, they often succumb. It is very probable that in their old mode of life they were rarely ill, but at the misiones the great change in their habits, the different kind of nourishment now partaken of, the restrictions of compulsory labor, together with other matters, are probably the principal causes of early deaths among them. The religiosos find fault because the Indians, upon the slightest illness, become wholly cast down and dejected, and, surrendering themselves to this depression of spirits, will not respect either the diet or anything else recommended for their recovery. With the exception of some simple emetics and cathartics which they keep for their own use, the misioneros are unprovided with medicaments.

The measles had been very general here for some months, with fatal results to the Indians, and some thousands of them in Nueva California died of the disease. But the Spaniards, who had also caught the infection, recovered without any further evil consequences. It seems that the main pores of the Indians are closed, and hence the eruption does not easily break out. This results in a severe fever of a lingering and malignant character. Almost every pregnant Indian woman that was infected with the disease miscarried.

The most terrible disease of all those prevailing here is that one known all over the globe—venereal. It is universal, both among the Spaniards and the Indians, and occasions so much the greater ravage because those infected reject all medical aid in its cure. Spots upon the skin, hard swellings, pains in the bones, inflammations of the throat, loss of the nose, consumption, and death, are the inevitable and usual consequences. Ophthalmia, rheumatic pains, swellings at the corner of the mouth, as well as chronic diseases of many sorts coming under my observation, may also, I believe, be pretty generally referred to the same origin.

Otto von Kotzebue (1787–1846) spent a month in San Francisco Bay in 1816 while on the first of two around-the-world voyages of exploration. The Spanish were friendly and hospitable, and although the Russians' visit was a pleasant one, Kotzebue found little to like. The natives were stupid and ugly, the Spanish soldiers were destitute, and the Franciscan friars (whom he referred to as "monks") failed to teach and train the Indians.

The best result for the preservation of California history was that the expedition produced three important books: Kotzebue's three-volume work, from which these excerpts are taken; a two-volume work by Adelbert von Chamisso, the French-born naturalist of the expedition; and an impressive illustrated volume by Louis Choris, the expedition's artist. Two of the illustrations (originally in color) from his volume, *Voyage Pittoresque autour de Monde,* are reproduced in this chapter.

Otto von Kotzebue

From:
A Voyage of Discovery into the South Sea and Beering's
Straits, for the purpose of exploring a North-East Pas-
sage, undertaken in the Years 1815–1818 . . . *in the ship
Rurick . . . .*

A low ridge of mountains borders the coast of
California, where we saw it [near Santa Barbara], and intercepts the prospect into the interior of the country. . . . The harbour of San Francisco . . .
enters through a narrow passage, receives some rivers from the interior,
branches out behind the eminences, and forms into a peninsula, the country lying south of the entrance. The Presidio and the Mission of San
Francisco lie on this tongue of land, which, with its hills and downs, was
the narrow field which lay immediately open to our researches. . . .

The environs of San Francisco, in the norther hemisphere, are much
poorer in natural productions than the coast of Chili, under the same
latitude, in the southern. In the spring, when winter has afforded the earth
some moisture, the hills and valleys are indeed adorned with brilliant iris
and other flowers; but the drought soon destroys them.

The fogs, which the prevailing sea-winds blow over the coast, dissolve
in summer over a heated and parched soil, and the country exhibits in
autumn only the prospect of bare scorched tracts, alternating with poor
stunted bushes, and in places, with dazzling wastes of drift sand. Dark
pine forests appear here and there on the ridge of the mountains, between
the Punta de los Reyes and the harbour of San Francisco. The prickly-
leafed oak, *Quercus agrifolia,* is the most common and largest tree. With
crooked boughs and entangled branches, it lies, like the other bushes, bent
towards the land; and the flattened tops, swept by the sea-wind, seem to
have been clipped by the gardener's shears. The Flora of this country is

View of the Presidio, San Francisco, 1816, by Louis Choris.

poor, and is not adorned by one of those species of plants which are produced by a warmer sun. . . .

Melancholy feelings attend our offering a few words on the Spanish settlements on this coast. With an avaricious thirst for possession, Spain extends her territory here, merely because she envies others the room. She maintains her Presidios at a great expence, and tries, by the prohibition of all trade, to force ready money back to its source. But a little liberty would make California the granary and market of the northern coasts of these seas, and the general resort of the ships which navigate them. . . .

Yet California lies without industry, trade, and navigation, desert and unpeopled. It has remained neglected, without any importations from Mexico, during the six or seven years of the war between Spain and its colonies. The ship from St. Blas, which formerly brought supplies to these settlements yearly, arrived in Monterey only while we were there. The missions possess some bad barks in the harbour of San Francisco, built by foreign captives. Even the Presidio has not a single boat; and other havens are no better off. . . .

But the maintenance of this colony is ascribed to another motive besides policy: namely, the pious intention of propagating the Christian religion, and the conversion of heathen nations. The governor of the province himself, informed us, that this was the real state of the case. Well then, a good work has been here injudiciously begun and ill-executed.

The pious Franciscans, who hold the missions in New California, are not skilled in the arts and trades which they ought to exercise and teach, nor in any of the languages spoken by the nations to whom they are sent. They are monks, exactly like those in the convents of Europe.[1] They direct a considerable agricultural establishment; (always two in each mission,) perform divine service, and converse with those committed to their charge, by means of interpreters, who are themselves Indians. All property belongs to the community of the mission, and is administered by the fathers. The savage Indian derives no immediate advantage from his labours; no wages, if he happens to be let out as a day-labourer on the Presidio. The mission receives the money which he earns. He acquires no notion of property, and is not bound by it. We do not deny the mildness, the paternal anxiety of the missionaries, of which we have several times

---

1. Kotzebue's footnote: We were more offended than edified by a sermon preached in the Spanish language, in the mission of San Francisco, on the Saint's day; and in which the patron saint was placed on an equality with Christ.

been witnesses. The relation still remains what is here represented; and, in our opinion, it would differ only in name, if the master of slaves kept them to work, and let them out at pleasure, he also would give them food.

The savage comes unthinkingly into the mission, receives the food which is willingly offered him, and listens to the instructions: he is still free. But as soon as he is baptized, he belongs to the church; and hence he looks with pain and longing to his native mountains. The church has an inalienable right to her children, and exercises this right with rigour.

The savage is inconsiderate and inconstant, like a child. Work, to which he is unaccustomed, is too difficult for him; he repents of the step which binds him, and demands his pristine liberty. The love of home, is, in him, a ruling passion. The fathers allow their Indians, for the most part, twice a year, a leave of absence for some weeks to visit their friends, and their native place.[2] On occasion of these journeys, which are undertaken in companies, apostates fall off, and new converts come in. The first, some of whom become the bitterest enemies to the Spaniards, the missionaries endeavour, on their excursions, to regain by gentle means; and if they do not succeed, they have recourse to the armed force. Hence many of the hostile events between the Spaniards and Indians.

The Indians die in the missions, in an alarming and increasing proportion. San Francisco contains about a thousand Indians: the number of deaths, in the last year, exceeded three hundred; it amounts already this year, (till October,) to two hundred and seventy, of which forty occurred during the last month. . . .

There is no medical assistance here, except bleeding, which is said to have been taught them by a ship's surgeon; and this remedy being since applied on every occasion, is more fatal than advantageous. Particularly one disorder, which, though the opinions are divided, has probably been spread by the Europeans, carries off its victims without opposition. It likewise prevails among the savage tribes: these latter do not, however,

---

2. Kotzebue's footnote: Two sick people, a man and his wife, whose end seemed to be fast approaching, being unable to undertake the journey, had remained behind the throng of departing Indians. They did not return to the mission; they laid themselves naked as they were on the damp ground, on the shore near our tents, without a covering from the stormy rainy nights. Their looks were fixed on their blue mountains; they saw their native home; and thus consoled themselves for not being able to reach it. The fathers after a few days, observing them, sent them back into the mission, addressing them with much mildness.

Dance of the Inhabitants of California at the Mission of San Francisco, 1816, by Louis Choris.

disappear from the earth with the same dreadful rapidity. The number of the whites, on the other hand, increases.

The contempt which the missionaries have for the people, to whom they are sent, seems to us, considering their pious occupation, a very unfortunate circumstance. None of them appear to have troubled themselves about their history, customs, religions, or languages: "They are irrational savages, and nothing more can be said of them. Who would trouble himself with their stupidity? who would spend his time upon it?"

In fact, these tribes are far below those on the north coast, and the interior of America. In their general appearance, they resemble each other, except the Tcholovonians, whom we soon learnt to distinguish by their marked physiognomy, which the fathers could not do. Their flat, broad countenance, with large staring eyes, is shaded by black, thick, long, and smooth hair. The gradations of color, the languages, which are radically different from each other; the mode of life, arts, arms, in some of them various lines tattoed about the chin and neck, the way in which they paint themselves for war and for the dance, distinguish the different tribes. They live among the Spaniards, and among themselves in different, friendly, or hostile relations. Among many of them their arms consist of bows and arrows; some of these are of extraordinary elegance, the bows light and strong, and covered with the sinews of animals on the convex side; among others it is merely of wood, and rudely made: some possess the art (women's work) of constructing neat and water-proof vessels of coloured blades of grass; but the Indian, for the most part, forgets his industry in the missions. They all go naked. They do not possess horses or canoes of any kind; they only know how to fasten together bundles of rushes, which carry them over the water by their comparative lightness. Those who live near rivers subsist principally on salmon, which they catch in baskets; those in the mountains on wild fruits and grain. They neither sow nor reap, but burn their meadows from time to time to increase their fertility.

. . . A fort, erected in a good situation, guards the harbour of San Francisco. The Presidio is new built with stone, and covered with tiles. The building of the chapel has not yet been begun. In the missions they build in the same manner, and the barracks of the Indians at San Francisco are of similar construction. An artillerist has erected mills in the missions, worked by horses; but they are now for the most part out of order, and cannot be repaired. At San Francisco is a stone which a horse turns without mechanism over another stone, the only mill in order. The Indian women rub the corn between two stones for immediate use. A windmill of the Russian American Company's settlement creates astonishment, but does not find imitators. Some years ago, when artizans were brought here at a great expense to teach the necessary arts, the Indians profited more by their instructions than the *gente rational* (rational people) as the Spaniards call themselves.[3]

We observed with regret, that the best understanding does not exist between the missions and the Presidio. The fathers consider themselves as the first in this country, and the Presidios merely sent for its protection. A soldier, who constantly carries and often uses arms, unwillingly bears the government of the church. The Presidios, living only on their pay, depend for the supply of their wants upon the missions, from which they purchase for ready money. They suffered distress in this latter period, neglected by the mother country, and accused the mission of not endeavouring to relieve them. Before we conclude, we must mention the generous hospitality with which both the military and the missionaries strove to supply our wants, and they willingly granted an unconstrained freedom, which we here enjoyed on Spanish ground. We dedicate these lines of remembrance and gratitude to our friends in California.

---

3. *Gente de razón* (People of reason) was a Spanish term that originally meant anyone with the least trace of white blood—to differentiate themselves from the Indians, who were considered to be no better than animals and thus without reason. At later times it came to be applied only to the ruling elite.

Camille de Roquefeuil of the French navy commanded the first French ship to enter San Francisco Bay—the *Bordelais,* a merchant vessel. Roquefeuil was on a commercial voyage to the Pacific, and was also circumnavigating the world—as everyone seemed to do at the time. The French were cordially received by the Spanish as fellow Catholics. They enjoyed the hospitality, made the obligatory visits to the presidio and the mission, and engaged in a bit of trade during a visit of only nine days.

Roquefeuil produced no new map, came away with no dramatic illustrations of early California, and indeed did not accomplished anything noteworthy other than to command the first French ship to make a commercial and political contact with the Spanish authorities in this remote part of the New World. But, almost inadvertently, he gave a precise and quite unpleasant report on the dreadful condition of the native population in upper and lower California.

Camille de Roquefeuil

From:
A Voyage Round the World Between the Years 1816–1819

My hopes of a fine passage to the coast of California were wholly disappointed; we had contrary and variable winds during the whole of July, the currents took us out of our course, and nothing occurred to break the monotony of this tiresome voyage. We did not see twenty birds during the whole month, and still fewer fish; whole weeks passed without seeing a living creature, so that we might have fancied ourselves alone in the creation. The appearance of a flying fish was an extraordinary occurrence. The month of August did not begin with better auspices; however, on the 3d we had some indications of the neighbourhood of land, and on the 5th, at two o'clock in the afternoon, we descried the coast of California. At five o'clock we perceived the port of St. Francisco, and soon after the fort, on the south east point of the entrance; we hoisted our colours and fired a gun, the fort did the same, hoisting the Spanish colours. The vessel entered rapidly with the tide; at six o'clock we passed under the fort; the officer hailed the ship, and we answered that she came from Lima. We ran into this basin, proceeding to the bay of Hyerba-Buena, where Vancouver first anchored. Just as we dropped anchor the ship touched the bottom, but without the slightest shock, as the ground was soft, and the next tide set us afloat again.

Two officers who had hailed us on the coast came on board in the boat, their names were Don Gabriel Moriaga [Moraga], (sub-lieutenant of cavalry, governor par interim of the Presidio,) and Don Manuel Gomez, lieutenant of artillery. These gentlemen were equally pleased and astonished to see us. No French vessel had ever before entered their port. They remained about an hour on board, partook of a little collation, and conversed with us in the most cordial manner. They did not appear to trouble themselves about politics, and had no knowledge of what was

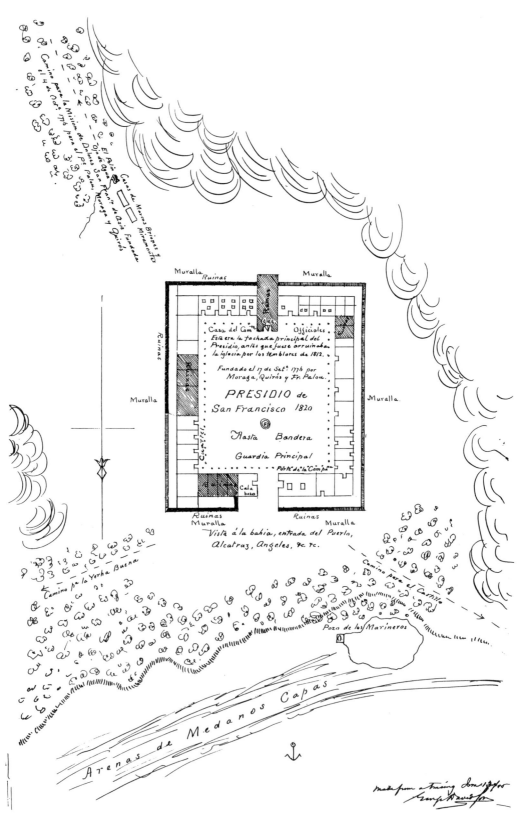

The Presidio of San Francisco in 1820.

North is toward the bottom. Several sections are in ruins, including the chapel. The trails to the mission, the Castillo, and Yerba Buena Cove are indicated. The houses of Marcos Briones and Miramontes are just southeast of the Presidio, near *El Polin Ojo de Agua*—a spring. *Pozo de los Marineros* is "Seamen's Well"—where ships could replenish their water supply.

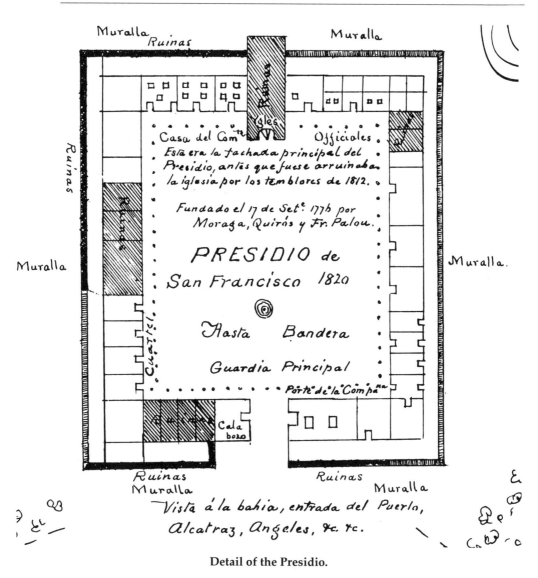

Muralla Ruinas   Muralla

Muralla

. Casa del Com^te   Officiales .
. Esta era la fachada principal del
. Presidio, antes que fuese arruinaba,
. la iglesia por los temblores de 1812. .

. Fundado el 17 de Set.^e 1776 por
. Moraga, Quirós y Fr. Palou. .

PRESIDIO de
San Francisco 1820

Hasta   Bandera

Guardia Principal

. . . . Porte de la Compa^ña .

Cala bozo

Ruinas   Ruinas
Muralla   Muralla

Muralla.

Vista á la bahía, entrada del Puerto,
Alcatraz, Angeles, &c. &c.

Detail of the Presidio.

Walls and ruins are labeled. At the top: House of the commandante, and houses of other officials.

"Here was the principal facade of the Presidio, before the church was destroyed by the earthquake of 1812. Founded on the 17th of September, 1776, by Moraga, Quirós, and Father Palou." From in front of the Presidio was a "view of the bay, the entrance to the port, Alcatraz and Angel islands, etc. etc."

passing in Chili. They told us that Mexico was almost entirely pacified; I learnt that there were but few furs in the country, an American, who left Monterey a fortnight before, having taken away the whole stock. Don Gabriel obligingly granted me permission to provide myself with the articles which I was in need of, and invited me to the Presidio.

The next day he sent horses for me and the surgeon. We rode four or five miles through a very uneven country, the horses galloping all the way, and entered the Presidio through the principal gate, where there is a guard. We alighted at the house of Don Gabriel, who, as well as his wife, received us with great politeness. Don Gabriel advised me to come and anchor at the Presidio, which I declined doing till I had seen the watering place; Don Manuel offered to accompany me to it. I found it inconvenient because it is some distance from the sea. Returning to Don Gabriel I met the father Ramon Abello, superior of the mission, whom I intended to visit. He congratulated me on my happy arrival, offered whatever his mission could afford, and said that he should be happy to see me there.

The road from the Presidio to the mission is over sand-hills, which produce only a coarse vegetation, ferns, stunted trees, pines, oaks, hollies, &c. This part was still more arid than the neighbourhood of our anchoring place. The mission is situated in an irregular valley between the hills on the north, and a small arm of the sea on the south. The soil seems much more fertile than at the Presidio, and the temperature is sensibly milder. The church is kept in good order, and handsomely decorated; the sacred utensils and the pictures are the work of Mexican artists, and exceed in richness and taste what is generally seen of this kind in most of the towns of the second and third rank in France and Germany: it may contain from 5 to 600 persons. There is not a single seat in it: the whole does credit to the piety and taste of the fathers: the Magazines well stored with corn, pease, &c.; the looms, in which cloth for the habits of the Indians is woven and the work-rooms, though not what might be desired, shew the industry and activity of these worthy men.

On going to pay another visit to the Presidio I met on the way Don Louis [Luis] Arguello, the governor, who used me very kindly, and promised to contribute all in his power to fulfil the object of my visit: I had some conversation with him on the interior of California and the Indians who inhabit it. He had ascended the San Sacramento to about fifty leagues from its mouth, and assured me that he had always found from seven to eight fathoms of water. The breadth of this river is very unequal, being two or three miles in some places, and not more than as many cables' lengths in others. In the rainy season it often overflows and covers the low country, on both sides, to the distance of three or four leagues from its mouth. This part, which is marshy and full of lagoons, is inhabited by Indians, who subsist upon fish. The interior is extremely fertile, the vine grows spontaneously, and though the grape is of inferior quality, for want of cultivation, Don Louis thought that brandy might be obtained from it. Maize hardly requires any attention. The savages, notwithstanding the inferiority of their arms, resist the parties which the Spaniards send at long intervals. If they are informed of their approach they abandon the villages, which are almost always found deserted, or occupied only by a few old people, who have not strength to fly. They lie in ambush and endeavour to surprize their enemy. In these incursions, the object of which is generally to look for natives who have deserted from the missions, it is very seldom that the Spaniards lose anybody, their jackets of buffalo's hide being a sufficient defence against the arrows of the savages.

After the accounts of La Peyrouse and Vancouver, and the complaints which the officers themselves made about the absolute want of workmen, I was surprised at seeing, in their houses, tables and benches of pretty good workmanship. On inquiring whence they obtained this furniture, Don Louis told me that they were the work of one of the Kodiaks, who had been taken prisoner while hunting the otter. Thus in an establishment formed forty years ago by Spain, a savage from the Russian possessions was the most skillful workman.

On the 10th, with most of the officers of the crew, I attended divine service at the Presidio, which was performed in a great hall, till the church, which had been burnt, should be rebuilt. This chapel, which was white washed and neatly kept, had an altar in pretty good taste, some pictures, and benches on the sides. Besides ourselves there were present about forty men, almost all military, and about a hundred women and children, all neatly dressed, and behaving with much decorum. . . . Father Ramon, who had officiated, invited us, as well as Don Louis, to dine at the mission. The repast, which was neatly served up, was composed of a small number of plain and substantial dishes, well dressed in the Spanish manner. The bread, meat, and vegetables were the produce of the mission, and of good quality. The conversation turned chiefly on the terrible decrease of the native race in the missions of the two Californias. They agreed that it was almost entirely extinct in old California; and for this reason the number of the missions was reduced from seven to two; it was also confessed that in the new province, which is more fertile, and was always more populous, there was not a single mission where the births were equal to the deaths.

Having taken leave of our kind friends, we set sail at five o'clock on the morning of the 14th of August.

Otto von Kotzebue returned to San Francisco Bay in 1826. His observations after an absence of eight years did not change his mind one whit from the opinions he acquired during his first visit.

Otto von Kotzebue

From:

A New Voyage Around the World in the Years 1823, 24, 25, and 26.

On the 25th of September we found ourselves, by observations, in the neighbourhood of the promontory called by the Spaniards "the King," not far from the bay of St. Francisco; but a thick fog, which at this season always reigns over the coast of California, veiled the wished-for land till the 27th. At ten o'clock in the morning of this day, at a distance of only three miles, we doubled his rocky majesty, a high bold hill terminating towards the sea in a steep wall of black rock, and having nothing at all regal in its appearance,—and perceived in his neighbourhood a very strong surf, occasioned by two contrary and violent currents raging, with the vain fury of insurrection, against the tranquillity of his immoveable throne.

The channel leading into the beautiful basin of St. Francisco is only half-gun shot wide, and commanded by a fortress situated on its left bank, on a high rock, named after St. Joachim. We could distinguish the republican flag, the waving signal, that even this most northern colony of Spain no longer acknowledges the authority of the mother country; we also remarked a few cavalry and a crowd of people who were watching our swiftly sailing vessel with the most eager attention. As we drew nearer, a sentinel grasped with both hands a long speaking trumpet, and enquired our nation and from whence we came. This sharp interrogatory, the sight of the cannon pointed upon our track, and the military, few indeed, but ready for battle, might have induced an opinion that the fortress had power to refuse entrance even to a ship of war, had we not been acquainted with the true state of affairs. St. Joachim, on his rocky throne, is truly a very peaceable and well-disposed saint; no one of his cannon is in condition to fire a single shot, and his troops are cautious of venturing into actual conflict; he fights with words only. I would not therefore refuse to his fortress the courtesy of a salute, but was much astonished at not finding my guns returned. An ambassador from shore soon solved the mystery, by coming to beg so much powder as would serve to answer my civility with becoming respect.

As soon as we had dropped anchor, the whole of the military left the fortress without a garrison, to mingle with the assemblage of curious gazers on the shore, where the apparition of our ship seemed to excite as much astonishment as in the South Sea Islands.

As our accounts of California are few and defective, a rapid glance at the history and constitution of this unknown but beautiful country, richly endowed by Nature with all that an industrious population could require to furnish the comforts and enjoyments of life, but hitherto sadly neglected under Spanish mis-government, will probably not be unwelcome to the readers who have accompanied me thus far.

The first missions were seated on the coast of Old California, for the convenience of communication by sea with Mexico, and because the country was favourable to agriculture. The military who accompanied the monks, selected for their residence a situation from whence they could overlook several missions, and be always ready for their defence. These military posts are here called Presidios.

As it was not possible to make the savage natives comprehend the doctrines of Christianity, their inculcation was out of the question; and all that these religionists thought necessary to be done with this simple, timid race, scarcely superior to the animals by whom they were surrounded, was to introduce the Catholic worship, or, more properly, the dominion of the monks, by force of arms. The missions multiplied rapidly. In new California, where we now were, the first of these, that of St. Diego, was established in 1769; now there are twenty-one in this country. Twenty-five thousand baptized Indians belong at present to these missions, and a military force of five hundred dragoons is found sufficient to keep them in obedience, to prevent their escape, or, if they should elude the vigilance of their guards, to bring them from the midst of their numerous tribes, improving the favourable opportunity of making new converts by the power of the sword.

The fate of these so called Christian Indians is not preferable even to that of negro slaves. Abandoned to the despotism of tyrannical monks, Heaven itself offers no refuge from their sufferings; for their spiritual masters stand as porters at the gate, and refuse entrance to whom they please. These unfortunate beings pass their lives in prayer, and in toiling for the monks, without possessing any property of their own. Thrice a day they are driven to church, to hear a mass in the Latin language; the rest of their time is employed in labouring in the fields and gardens with coarse, clumsy implements, and in the evening they are locked up in over-crowded barracks, which, unboarded, and without windows or beds, rather resemble cows' stalls than habitations for men. A coarse woollen shirt which they make themselves, and then receive as a present from the missionaries, constitutes their only clothing. Such is the happiness which the Catholic religion has brought to the uncultivated Indian; and this is the paradise which he must not presume to undervalue by attempting a return to freedom in the society of his unconverted countrymen, under penalty of imprisonment in fetters.

Frederick William Beechey (1796–1856) was an English naval officer and geographer. In 1825 he was put in command of the sloop *Blossom*, with instructions to explore Bering Strait and to cooperate with the expeditions of Franklin and Parry, which entered the Arctic from the south and east. Beechey passed through the strait and went beyond 71° N.

As winter approached, the *Blossom* sailed southward and entered San Francisco Bay on November 6, 1826. Since Beechey's duties included making surveys in the Pacific, he engaged in that activity during the seven weeks he was in the bay. It was the first scientific survey of the bay, and produced charts that were still the best existing ones into the American period; they were not superseded until those produced by Cadwalader Ringgold of the 1841 United States Exploring Expedition, published in 1851. And even those charts owed much to Beechey.

Beechey transferred the name *Isla de Alcatraces* (Pelican Island) from present Yerba Buena Island, where it had been placed by Ayala in 1775, to its present location—as "Los Alcatrazes." There is no indication whether this was accidental or intentional. He discovered the barely submerged "Blossom Rock"—named after his ship—a navigational hazard that was dynamited in 1870 by A. W. von Schmidt.

Beechey's survey covered all of San Francisco and San Pablo bays, and as far as Carquinez Strait; the information on his chart beyond that point was received at second hand. There are two charts—one of the entire bay and the other of the entrance to the bay.

Captain Frederick William Beechey

From:
Narrative of a Voyage to the Pacific and
Beering's Strait . . . in the Years 1825, 26, 27, 28.

When the day broke, we found ourselves about four miles from the land. It was a beautiful morning, with just sufficient freshness to the air to exhilarate without chilling. The tops of the mountains, the only part of the land visible, formed two ranges, between which our port was situated, through its entrance, as well as the valleys and the low lands, were still covered with the morning mist condensed around the bases of the mountains. We bore up for the opening between the ranges, anxious for the rising sun to withdraw the veil, that we might obtain a view of the harbour, and form our judgment of the country in which we were about to pass the next few weeks. As we advanced, the beams of the rising sun gradually descended the hills, until the mist, dispelled from the land, rolled on before the refreshing sea wind, discovering cape after cape, and exhibiting a luxuriant country apparently abounding in wood and rivers. At length two low promontories, the southern one distinguished by a fort and a Mexican flag, marked the narrow entrance of the port.

We spread our sails with all the anxiety of persons who had long been secluded from civilized society, and deprived of wholesome aliment; but after the first effort of the breeze, it died away and left us becalmed in a heavy N. W. swell.

At length a breeze sprung up, and we entered the port, and dropped our anchor in the spot where Vancouver had moored his ship thirty-three years before.

The Port of San Francisco does not show itself to advantage until after the fort is passed, when it breaks upon the view, and forcibly impresses the spectator with the magnificence of the harbour. He then beholds a broad sheet of water, sufficiently extensive to contain all the British navy, with convenient coves, anchorage in every part, and, around, a country diversified with hill & dale, partly wooded and partly disposed in pasture lands of the richest kind, abounding in herds of cattle. In short, the only objects wanting to complete the interest of the scene are some useful establishments and comfortable residences on the grassy borders of the harbour, the absence of which creates an involuntary regret that so fine a country, abounding in all that is essential to man, should be allowed to remain in such a state of neglect. So poorly did the place appear to be peopled that a sickly column of smoke rising from within some dilapidated walls, misnamed the presidio or protection, was the only indication we had of the country being inhabited.

As we opened out the several islands and stopping places in the harbour, we noticed seven American whalers at anchor at Sausalito, not one of which showed their colours; we passed them and anchored off a small bay named Yerba Buena, from the luxuriance of its vegetation, about a league distant from both the presidio and the mission of San Francisco.

We were happy to find the country around our anchorage abounding in game of all kinds, so plentiful, indeed, as soon to lessen the desire of pursuit; still there were many inducements to both the officers and seamen to land and enjoy themselves; and as it was for the benefit of the service that they should recruit their health and strength as soon as possible, every facility was afforded them. Horses were fortunately very cheap, from nine shillings to seven pounds apiece, so that riding became a favorite amusement; and the Spaniards finding they could make a good market by letting out their stud, appeared with them every Sunday opposite the ship, ready saddled for the occasion, as this was the day on which I allowed every man to go out of the ship. Some of the officers purchased horses and tethered them near the place, but the Spaniards finding this to interfere with their market, contrived to let them loose on the Saturday night, in order that the officers might be compelled to hire others on the following day.

Such of the seaman as would not venture on horseback made parties to visit the presidio and mission, where they found themselves welcome guests with the Spanish soldiers. These two places were the only buildings within many miles of us, and they fortunately supplied just enough spirits to allow the people to enjoy themselves with their friends, without indulging in much excess—a very great advantage in a seaport.

The governor's abode was in a corner of the presidio, and formed one end of a row, of which the other was occupied by a chapel; the opposite side was broken down, and little better than a heap of rubbish and bones, on which jackals, dogs, and vultures were constantly preying; the other

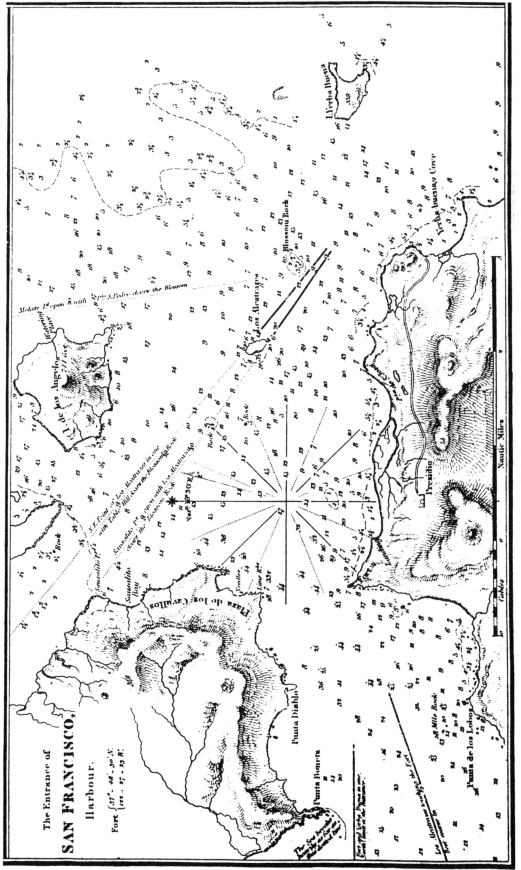

Beechey's chart of The Entrance of San Francisco Harbour, at full size. The trail from Yerba Buena Cove to the Presidio is shown, as is the lagoon at the foot of where Sacramento Street was later located.

two sides of the quadrangle contained storehouses, artificer's shops, and the gaol, all built in the humblest style with badly burnt bricks, and roofed with tiles. The chapel & the governor's house were distinguished by being whitewashed.

Morning and evening mass are daily performed in the missions, and high mass as it is appointed by the Romish church, at which all the converted Indians are obliged to attend. The commemoration of the anniversary of the patroness saint took place during my visit at San Jose, and high mass was celebrated in the church. Before the prayers began, there was a procession of the young female Indians, with which I was highly pleased. They were neatly dressed in scarlet petticoats & white bodices, and walked in a very orderly manner to the church, where they had places assigned to them apart from the males. After the bell had done tolling, several alguazils[1] went round to the huts to see if all the Indians were at church, and if they found any loitering within them, they exercised with tolerable freedom a long lash with a broad thong at the end of it; a discipline which appeared the more tyrannical, as the church was not sufficiently capacious for all the attendants, and several sat upon the steps without; but the Indian women who had been captured in the affair with the Cosemenes were placed in a situation where they could see the costly images, and vessels of burning incense, and every thing that was going forward.

The congregation was arranged on both sides of the building, separated by a wide aisle passing along the centre, in which were stationed several alguazils with whips, canes, and goads to preserve silence and maintain order, and, what seemed more difficult than either, to keep the congregation in their kneeling posture. The goads were better adapted to this purpose than the whips, as they would reach a long way, and inflict a sharp puncture without making any noise. The end of the church was occupied by a guard of soldiers under arms with fixed bayonets; a precaution which I suppose experience had taught the necessity of observing. Above them there was a choir consisting of several Indian musicians, who performed very well indeed on various instruments, and sang the Te Deum in a very passable manner. The congregation was very attentive, but the gratifica-

---

1. An *alguazil* is, literally, a bailiff—one who keeps order in a courtroom. The word is still in use in modern Spanish. Here it is used to indicate a kind of policeman or overseer, one who enforces the rules both in and out of church.

tion they appeared to derive from the music furnished another proof of the strong hold this portion of the ceremonies of the Romish church takes upon uninformed minds.

The only amusement which my hospitable host of the mission of San Jose indulged in during my visit to that place, was during meal times, when he amused himself by throwing pancakes to the *muchachos*, a number of little Indian domestics who stood gaping round the table. For this purpose, he had every day two piles of pancakes made of Indian corn; and as soon as the olla was removed, he would fix his eyes upon one of the boys, who immediately opened his mouth, and the padre, rolling up a cake, would say something ludicrous in allusion to the boy's appetite, or to the size of his mouth, and pitch the cake at him, which the imp would catch between his teeth, and devour with incredible rapidity, in order that he might be ready the sooner for another, as well as to please the padre, whose amusement consisted in a great measure in witnessing the sudden disappearance of the cake. In this manner the piles of cakes were gradually distributed among the boys, amidst much laughter and occasional squabbling.

Nothing could exceed the kindness and consideration of these excellent men to their guests and to travellers, and they were seldom more pleased than when any one paid their mission a visit: we always fared well there, and even on fast days were provided with fish dressed in various ways, and preserves made with the fruit of the country. We had, however, occasionally some difficulty in maintaining our good temper, in consequence of the unpleasant remarks which the difference of our religion brought from the padres, who were very bigoted men, and invariably introduced this subject. At other times they were very conversible, and some of them were ingenious and clever men; but they had been so long excluded from the civilized world that their ideas & their politics, like the maps pinned against the walls, bore date of 1772, as near as I could read it for fly spots. Their geographical knowledge was equally backward, as my host at San Jose had never heard of the discoveries of Captain Cook; and because Otaheite[2] was not placed upon his chart, he would scarcely credit its existence.

The Indians after their conversion are quiet and tractable, but extremely indolent, and given to intoxication, and other vices. Gambling in particular they indulge in to an unlimited extent: they pledge the very clothes on

2. Tahiti.

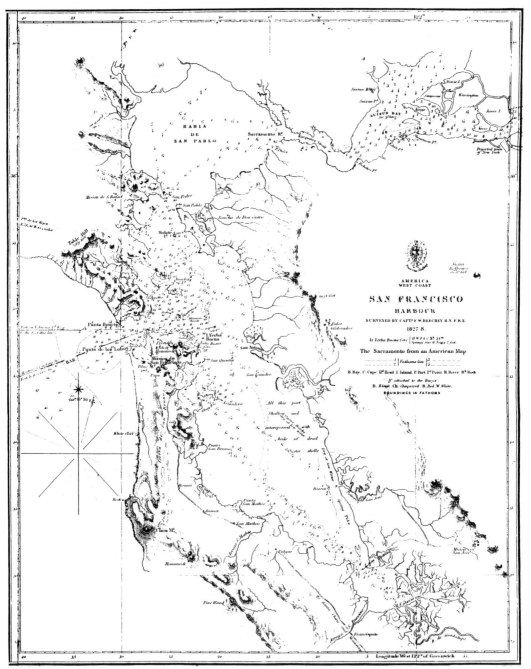

Beechey's chart of San Francisco Harbour.
At right center, Sierra Bolbones is Mount Diablo. At left center, Table Hill is Mount Tamalpais.

their backs, and not infrequently have been known to play for each other's wives.

Formerly the missions had small villages attached to them, in which the Indians lived in a very filthy state; these have almost all disappeared since Vancouver's visit, and the converts are disposed of in huts as before described; and it is only when sickness prevails to a great extent that it is necessary to erect these habitations, in order to separate the sick from those who are in health. Sickness in general prevails to an incredible extent in all the missions, and on comparing the census of the years 1786 and 1813, the proportion of deaths appears to be increasing. At the former period there had been only 7,701 Indians baptized, out of which 2,388 had died; but in 1813 there had been 37,437 deaths to only 57,328 baptisms.

The Indians in general submit quietly to the discipline of the missions, yet insurrections have occasionally broken out, particularly in the early stage of the settlement, when father Tamoral and other priests suffered martyrdom. In 1823, also, a priest was murdered in a general insurrection in the vicinity of San Luis Rey; and in 1827, the soldiers of the garrison were summoned to quell another riot in the same quarter.

[In the following paragraphs, Beechey compiled a narrative from the journals of three of his officers, who traveled by land to Monterey to learn whether certain supplies could be procured for the ship. A portion of the narrative is included here for its description of the terrain from Yerba Buena Cove to the mission and thence south down the peninsula.]

In order to reach a tolerable halting place for the night, the first day's journey was necessarily long, and consequently by daylight on the 9th of November the three officers were on their road to the mission; having found horses and an escort prepared in pursuance of previous arrangements.

Setting off at a round trot, they made the best of their way over three or four miles of ground so overgrown with dwarf oaks and other trees that they were every moment in danger of being thrown from their horses, or having their eyes torn out by the branches as they passed. In half an hour, however, they reached the mission of San Francisco, and soon forgot the little annoyances they had hitherto met, in the hospitable welcome of the good priest, who regaled them with excellent pears and new milk.

Leaving the mission of San Francisco, the party receded from the only part of the country that is wooded for any considerable distance, and ascended a chain of hills about a thousand feet in height, where they had an extensive view, comprehending the sea, the Farallones rocks, and the distant Punta de los Reyes, a headland so named by the expedition under

Sebastian Viscaino in 1602. The ridge which afforded this wide prospect was called Sierra de San Bruno, and for the most part was covered with a burnt-up grass; but such places as were bare presented to the eye of the geologist rocks of sandstone conglomerate, intersected by a few veins of jaspar. Winding through the Sierra de San Bruno, they crossed a river of that name, and opened out the broad arm of the sea which leads from the port to Santa Clara, and is confined between the chain they were traversing and the Sierra de los Bolbones,[3] distinguishable at a distance by a peaked mountain 3,783 feet high by trigonometrical measurement. Upon the summit of that part of the sierra bordering the arm of sea called Estrecho de San Jose, a thick wood, named Palos Colorados from its consisting principally of red cedar pine, stands conspicuous on the ridge. I mention this particularly, and wish to call attention to the circumstance, as the straggling trees at the south extreme of the wood are used as landmarks for avoiding a dangerous rock which we discovered in the harbour, and named after the Blossom.

About noon they reached a small cottage named Burri Burri, about twelve miles from San Francisco.... From Burri Burri, a continuation of the Sierra de San Bruno passes along the centre of the peninsula formed by the sea and the Estrecho de San Jose, and is separated from this arm of the harbour by a plain, upon which the travellers now descended from the mountains, and journeyed at a more easy and agreeable rate than they had done on the rugged paths among the hills. This plain near the sea is marshy, and having obtained the name of Las Salinas is probably overflowed occasionally by the sea.

Travelling onward, the hills on their right, known in that part as the Sierra del Sur, began to approach the road, which passing over a small eminence, opened out upon a wide country of meadow land, with clusters of fine oak free from underwood. It strongly resembled a nobleman's park: herds of cattle and horses were grazing upon the rich pasture, and numerous fallow-deer, startled at the approach of strangers, bounded off to seek protection among the hills. The resemblance, however, could be traced no further. Instead of a noble mansion, in character with so fine a country, the party arrived at a miserable mud dwelling, before the door of which a number of half-naked Indians were basking in the sun. Several dead geese, deprived of their entrails, were fixed upon pegs around a large pole, for the purpose of decoying the living game into snares, which were placed

---

3. Mount Diablo

The Mission of San Francisco, Upper California, in 1826, by William Smyth. From a lithograph in *California: A History of Upper and Lower California*, 1839, by Alexander Forbes.

for them in favourable situations. Heaps of bones also of various animals were lying about the place, and sadly disgraced the park-like scenery around. This spot is named San Matheo, and belongs to the mission of San Francisco.

*   *   *   *   *   *   *   *   *   *   *

By Christmas day we had all remained sufficiently long in the harbour to contemplate our departure without regret: the eye had become familiar to the picturesque scenery of the bay, the pleasure of the chase had lost its fascination, and the roads to the mission and presidio were grown tedious and insipid. There was no society to enliven the hours, no incidents to vary one day from the other, and to use the expression of Donna Gonzales, California appeared to be as much out of the world as Kamschatka.

On the 26th, being ready for sea, I was obliged to relinquish the survey of this magnificent port, which possesses almost all the requisites for a great naval establishment, and is so advantageously situated with regard to North America and China, and the Pacific in general, that it will, no doubt, at some future time, be of great importance. We completed the examination of those parts of the harbour which were likely to be frequented by vessels for some years to come, in which it is proper to mention, in order to give as much publicity to the circumstance as possible, that we discovered a rock between Alcatrasses & Yerba Buena Islands, dangerous to both shipping and boats, in consequence of its rising from about seven fathoms so near to the surface, as to occasion strong overfalls with the tides. A shoal was also found to the eastward of the landing-place off the presidio, which ought to be avoided by boats sailing along shore. In my nautical remarks I purpose giving directions for avoiding both these dangers, which are the only hidden ones in that part of the harbour which is at present frequented.

On the 28th, we took leave of our hospitable and affable friends, Martinez and Padre Tomaso, full of gratitude for their kindness and attention to our wants; weighed anchor, and bade adieu to the Port of San Francisco, in which we had all received material benefit from the salubrity of its climate, the refreshing product of its soil, and the healthy exercise we had enjoyed there. In the ship's company in particular there was the most apparent amendment; some of them, from being so emaciated on their arrival that the surgeon could scarcely recognize them, were now restored to their former healthy appearance, and we had the satisfaction of sailing without a single case of sickness on board.

*   *   *   *   *   *   *   *   *   *   *

The more we became acquainted with the beautiful country around San Francisco, the more we were convinced that it possessed every requisite to render it a valuable appendage to Mexico; and it was impossible to resist joining in the remark of Vancouver, "Why such an extent of territory should have been subjugated, and, after all the expense and labour bestowed upon its colonization, turned to no account whatever, is a mystery in the science of state policy not easily explained." Situated in the northern hemisphere, between the parallels of 22° and 39°, no fault can be found with its climate; its soil in general is fertile, it possesses forests of oak and pine convenient for building and contributing to the necessities of vessels, plains overrun with cattle, excellent ports, and navigable rivers to facilitate inland communication. Possessing all these advantages, an industrious population alone seems requisite to withdraw it from the obscurity in which it has so long slept under the indolence of the people and the jealous policy of the Spanish government. Indeed it struck us as lamentable to see such an extent of habitable country lying almost desolate and useless to mankind, whilst other nations are groaning under the burthen of their population.

It is evident, from the natural course of events, and from the rapidity with which observation has recently been extended to the hitherto most obscure parts of the globe, that this indifference cannot continue; for either it must disappear under the present authorities, or the country will fall into other hands, as from its situation in regard to other powers upon the new continent, and to the commerce of the Pacific, it is of too much importance to be permitted to remain long in its present neglected state. Already have the Russians encroached upon the territory by possessing themselves of the Farallones, and some islands off Santa Barbara; and their new settlement at Rossi, a few miles to the northward of Bodega, is so near upon the boundary as to be the cause of much jealous feeling—not without reason it would appear, as I am informed it is well fortified, and presents to California an example of what may be effected upon her shores in a short time by industry.

Auguste Bernard Duhaut-Cilly (1790–1849) differed from most of the early foreign visitors to San Francisco Bay in that he was a captain in the merchant marine in command of a ship, the *Héros*, engaged in a commercial enterprise rather than one of exploration, mapping, or other scientific or political endeavor.

Essentially he was on this part of the Pacific coast of America to negotiate for hides and tallow, as were others—mainly Americans—at the same time. He was cordially received by the Spanish, probably because he was a fellow Catholic.

Duhaut-Cilly was an astute observer and excelled at describing what he had seen—and also seemed to have considered himself something of a ladies' man: suave, genteel, flirtatious—but always in control of the situation, as befits a man who is considerably above those whom he observes.

An English translation of a portion of Duhaut-Cilly's *Voyage* was published as "Duhaut-Cilly's Account of California" in three successive issues of the *California Historical Society Quarterly* in 1929. Excerpts from that account are reprinted here with the permission of the California Historical Society.

From:
Voyage autour du monde . . . en 1826, 1827, 1828, 1829.

Auguste Bernard Duhaut-Cilly

The morning of the 26th [of January] we had, at last, clear weather; and as soon as it was light, we made out the entrance to the port of San Francisco, distant about three leagues. The view agreed perfectly with Vancouver's description: the northern coast presented steep walls of rock of a violet color; and the lower southern coast was composed of sand-dunes mixed with large scattered rocks, some of which projected several hundred metres into the sea at the entrance to the channel.

We had a good breeze, and we wasted no time in passing through the narrow channel leading to the great harbor of San Francisco. After passing the first point where are the rocks I have just mentioned, we reached another, more elevated, on which is built an old Spanish fort; and almost at once we found ourselves opposite a cluster of houses which all of us took for a farm; but on examining them more closely, and consulting the accounts of the navigators I have lately cited, Vancouver and Roquefeuille, I recognized the presidio. Since everything was ready for anchoring, we had only to change our course, steering the ship toward the gentle curve taken by the southern shore just beyond the fort; and at the end of a few minutes, the lead showing seventeen fathoms and a mud bottom, we let go the anchor, two hundred fathoms from the beach.

Some men on horseback rushed at once to the shore. I landed with M. ——, and we encountered some soldiers who offered us horses and invited us to go to the presidio. We set out, making a long detour in order to avoid some marshes that we had not noticed from the ship, and after a quarter of an hour we came to the house of the commandant, Don Ignacio Martinez, lieutenant of infantry, who welcomed us very courteously, congratulated us on our arrival, and placed himself and all he possessed at our service—a hollow Spanish expression that doesn't mean anything.

Don Ignacio Martinez had a large family, in particular many young girls of very pleasing appearance, several of whom were already married. The husband of one of these young persons was an Englishman, named Richardson, who appeared to me to be very well acquainted with the harbor and the outside coast. He corroborated the Russian captain's opinion upon the passage between the Farallones and Point Reyes, and assured me that there was no danger. He told me also that we had chosen a poor anchorage, and he offered to pilot the ship to that of Yerba Buena, situated in a cove farther inland, behind a large point that could be seen a league to the east.

During this conversation, which took place in Don Ignacio's reception room, we heard a volley of seven guns coming from the *Héros,* which I had directed to be given only when it should be estimated that I had reached the presidio—for I wished to see what effect this courtesy would have upon the commandant of San Francisco.

As soon as I had told him that this was intended for him, he seemed to grow a foot taller; and I noticed that several soldiers and individuals, who until that moment had remained covered, respectfully took off their hats. He gave orders at once to his daughters, to some to fetch cheese, to others, *tortillas* and cakes; to these, some sweet wine from Mission San Luis Rey, to those, brandy from San Luis Obispo. All obeyed with an eagerness that could be translated thus: "Papa must be a very great man, since they fire seven guns in his honor." Everything within was in confusion while he sent a corporal to the fort to attempt to return at least a part of the salute. But of the seven pieces that were loaded, only three were heard to be fired. Nonetheless, this cost the Mexican government two gun carriages that the explosions reduced to powder—followed by more excuses from Don Ignacio.

The loss of two old engines of war did not prevent us from profiting from the attentions of our pretty Californians. Their bloom, their liveliness hardly restrained by the presence of strangers, pleased us, and this frame of mind contributed not a little to make us find everything they offered us so delicious. The account we had just given them of the peril we had run into so near the port, had filled them with fright; one of them, in particular, seated in front of me, had suddenly grown pale in a remarkable manner. "Do you think," I said to her, "it is buying too dearly the pleasure of eating *tortillas* made by your pretty hands?" She cast down her eyes, and her pallor withdrew before a more pronounced shade.

At last we returned to the ship with Richardson, and we found at the anchorage the Russian brig, which had just arrived.

We veered at once on our anchor chain; but before we were directly over the anchor, we saw floating on the water the anchor-stock, which the force of the ebb-tide, against a stiff breeze from the west-northwest that kept the ship broadside to the wind, had broken. This accident, which could have easily been repaired, did not, unhappily, stop here, for on raising the anchor we found it with one fluke broken off. We had lost the third anchor in one of the outside moorings, so that this new misfortune left us henceforth with only two anchors, without knowing when or how we could procure others.

We got under way, nevertheless, and proceeded slowly against a rushing current, which a strong breeze could scarcely overcome. At first we went two miles to the east, going along quite near the coast; then a mile east 15° south, at the end of which we reached the Yerba Buena cove, where we anchored in five fathoms, bottom of soft mud, the northern point of the cove entirely covering the entrance to the haven.

The next day, while the crew were busied in raising a tent in the most convenient spot on the shore, and in unloading the materials for building a whaling canoe that I had taken on board at Mazatlan, we went to pay a visit to the superior of Mission San Francisco, situated two miles from Yerba Buena.

I wanted to gain some information as to what success we could promise ourselves in this part of California, in order to decide upon our further plans. Fray Tomás[1] was expecting us; and he came to receive us with great demonstrations of friendship; a welcome which the behavior of this religious never, furthermore, belied in the numerous relations I later had with him.

Hardly were we seated around an oaken table, where we had *las once,*[2] than Fray Tomás asked me for news of Spain, in a tone betraying to me how greatly he regretted that California was no longer under the rule of that power. He was charmed, he told me, to find at last a Christian stranger with whom to converse; for all those heretics (meaning the English and Americans) open their mouths only to lie and to vomit blasphemy.

Notwithstanding this distinction, and the desire I had to tell him some-

---

1. Fray Tomás Eleuterio Esténega, who came to Mission San Francisco in October 1821.
2. A light repast of cakes, cheese, and drinks preceding the dinner, in order to sharpen the appetites of the guests.

thing satisfactory on the subject he had in mind, I could not hide from him the hardly prosperous condition his country was in when we left Europe. "But did not the French go to Spain to save Ferdinand and restore him to absolute power?" How, after that, make him understand that this claim to absolute power was actually the origin of all Spain's misery? I would have wasted my time, and I had not come to California to correct the political education of this worthy missionary.

I found Mission San Francisco very different from what it was when Vancouver visited it in 1794 [1792, correctly, when he described the mission. In 1794 Vancouver briefly was in Monterey, but did come to San Francisco Bay].

At that time it consisted of a chapel and a house forming two sides of a square. Not only has this square been completed since, but a large church and a row of fairly large buildings, serving as store-houses and dependencies, have been added to it.

Beyond this solid wall of buildings, separated from it by a large court where flows a stream of fine water, are the dwellings of the Indians attached to the mission. They are laid out in regular order, and separated by straight streets made at equal distances. This establishment became, some years ago, one of the most important in California, as much from the wealth of its products as from the number of its Indians. In 1827 there remained of this wealth only the numerous houses necessitated by it, and of which the larger number were already falling into ruin.

When Roquefeuille visited this mission in 1816, there were still seven hundred Indians; and when I arrived here there were not more than two hundred and sixty. . . .

The immense port of San Francisco is divided into two branches, one of which goes toward the north, the other toward the east-southeast. Each of these two inner bays measures nearly fifteen leagues in length, with a varying width of three to twelve miles. There are several islands in this great expanse of water, the largest of which is Los Angeles [Angel Island], north of the presidio.

Missions San Rafael and San Francisco Solano are on the borders of the northern bay; they are new and of slight importance.

On the shores of the eastern bay, beside Mission San Francisco with which the reader is already acquainted, are seen those of San José and of Santa Clara, the finest and richest in this part of California. Near Santa Clara is found also the pueblo of San José, which is only a big village.

. . . Bears are very common in the area; and without going farther than five or six leagues from San Francisco, they are often seen in herds, in the forests and even in the fields. The Californians claim that they seldom attack passers-by, and that only when one happens to be near them, or arouses their savageness by teasing them, do they make use of their terrible claws and their extraordinary strength. . . .

During our sojourn at Yerba Buena, we ordinarily went hunting during the many moments of leisure left us by our business, which was somewhat desultory and without consequence. The country supplied a large number of hares, rabbits, those tufted partridge, and particularly an astonishing variety of ducks and sea birds. All this for our table.

As for the collection I was engaged in creating with Dr. Botta, our quests were not less fruitful: on the seashore a swarm of beautiful shore birds; in the woods and on the hills, several fine species of hawk and other birds of prey; in the thickets, magpies, blackbirds, sparrows, and several fruit-eating birds all different from ours; finally, in the heath, a pretty species of hummingbird, perhaps the smallest existing, with a head and throat of glowing fire. . . .

On Sunday, with two officers from the ship and a guide, I went early to the mission, intending to make a hunting excursion to a place called Rancho de San Bruno, where we should find much game. But before going farther, we attended mass and heard a sermon from Fray Tomás on God's sixth commandment.

He handled his subject with talent; but I will confess that his discourse would have appeared very extraordinary to European ears accustomed to comprehend the periphrases usual in such matters; and though the good father had warned us, in his exordium, that one must not be afraid to speak plainly, without circumlocution, of the shamelessly committed offenses, he had to remind us that he was speaking to half-savage Indians, and to people almost as ignorant as they, in order to reconcile us to the *naïveté* of his imagery.

At last we mounted our horses and, for about three leagues, followed one side of a long valley, leaving, on the right hand and on the left, high verdant hills where the mission herds were grazing. At every moment we saw those animals that I have already described under the name of coyotes: their pelt is far from being as beautiful as that of the coyotes of Lower California; their color here tends much more to a dull grey; the tail is less covered with hair, and the fur is usually thinner.

When we reached the southern end of the valley we passed a ravine, and soon were in the plain, in the middle of which flows a brook, forming here and there little lakes. We dismounted on the edge of one of these ponds, and having tethered our horses, we went, each one by himself, to shoot the ducks of divers species, and the wild geese that we found in large numbers everywhere. Some of us also killed a species of heron, called in the country *grulla* [crane], considered a delicacy by the local people.

After spending three hours spreading terror and death among the hardly wild hosts of the air and the water, all of us returned, with more or less success, to the spot where we had left our steeds, supplied above all with great appetites, which we satisfied by means of the food with which we had been careful to provide ourselves.

In coming back we did not follow the route we had taken in the morning: we turned to the east and went round the hills that we had passed on our left. The slope of these hills is much greater on this side, which toward the harbor is almost vertical. One must have horses that are sure-footed and accustomed to venturing onto these *laderas* or narrow paths, hardly marked upon the mountain slope, and which leave frightful precipices below the rider, where the least slip would send him rolling with his horse to the edge of the steep wall of rock, and thence with one bound into the sea. . . .

Entrance to the Golden Gate (above), and looking out through the Golden Gate.
(Both illustrations are from *The Annals of San Francisco*.)

From the Spanish discovery of San Francisco Bay in 1769, to the establishment of the presidio and mission in 1776, and through the first third of the nineteenth century, the only entity anywhere in the San Francisco Bay region that could be called a town was the pueblo of San Jose. The mission and presidio each had a certain population attached to it—mainly an Indian population at the mission, mainly a Spanish and Mexican one at the presidio—but neither could be considered a town. Ships anchored just east of the presidio in the 'official' anchoring place, and from Vancouver in 1792 onward they increasingly anchored in Yerba Buena Cove, and also at Sausalito because of the better water supply there. But still there was no town on the shores of San Francisco Bay before 1835.

William Antonio Richardson (1795–1858), first mate on the British whaling ship *Orion*, arrived in California on August 2, 1822. As the result of a conflict with his captain, he jumped ship, became Catholicized, married a daughter of the *commandante* of the Presidio, and settled down to become one of the more prominent figures in the history of early California. He lived at the Presidio until 1829, and in San Gabriel from 1829 to 1835.

He was the founder and first resident of Yerba Buena—now San Francisco. Since he was one of the earliest on the scene, and was acquainted with events and the important people of the time, he was called upon to give testimony in federal district court in the 1850s concerning the Limantour and other land grant cases. To establish his *bona fides*, he was questioned at length about his role in the creation of the village of Yerba Buena.

William Antonio Richardson

The Founding of Yerba Buena

I went to see my father-in-law and arrived here with my family in June [1835], the latter part of the month, and pitched my tent here, to await the orders of General Figueroa.

He told me that he had seen a communication of mine to General Echandea respecting the Anchorage at Yerba Buena. He asked me if there was any spot sufficient to lay off a small village or town. I told him there was one abreast of the Anchorage where the vessels lay, a small place. He asked me the extent and wished me to give him a small sketch of it, which I did, stating the dimensions to the best of my knowledge of the clear spot. The sketch I gave[1] exhibited land and stated the extent to be about 400 varas[2] from the beach opposite the Anchorage in a southwest direction, and the direction of the valley runs about northwest and southeast about twelve hundred yards. I told him there were very few springs and it was very scarce of water. The land as above described as exhibited by the sketch was clear of bushes.

The first time I next heard from Monterey was from Don Francisco de Haro, Alcalde, then residing at the Mission of San Francisco de Assis.

He had a letter from the Political Government directing him to lay off a small village at Yerba Buena and to give me the first one hundred vara lot after the village was laid off. . . . I was then living in my tent in the hill at the edge of the woods within the limits of Yerba Buena. About two days after this he collected the ayuntamiento and came with them to my tent, and he told me he was then ready to lay off the village and required my

---

1. There are no existing copies of this original sketch of Yerba Buena.
2. A vara is thirty-three inches, and thus 400 varas is about 367 yards.

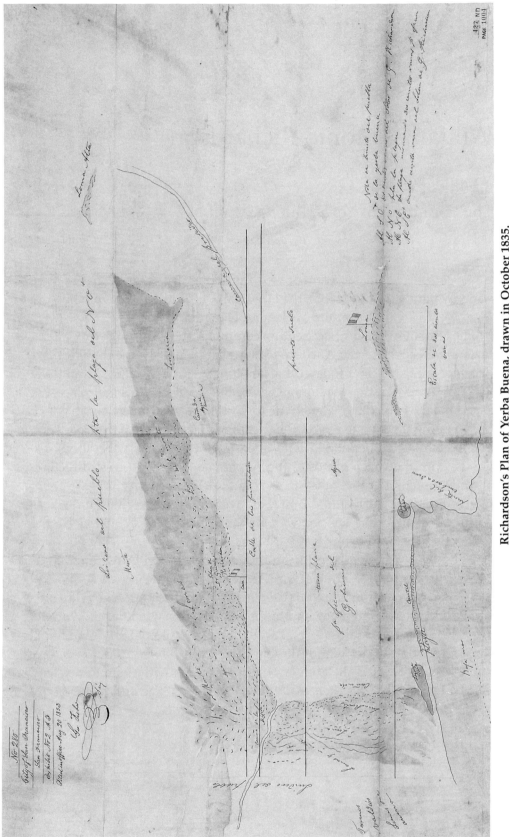

Richardson's Plan of Yerba Buena, drawn in October 1835.

It shows the town's single street—Calle de la Fundacion—and the single structure in the town, marked Casa and with a flag. The town's limits are shown, as are the roads to the presidio and the mission. "Loma Alta" at the upper right is Russian Hill, and the "Loma" with the flag on it is Telegraph Hill.

assistance in doing so. He told me his first orders were to reserve two hundred varas all along the beach opposite the anchorage for Government offices.

They measured off two hundred varas from the beach in a southwest direction and then told me that I could select some place out of that limit on the clear land for my own 100 vara lot. I told them that I wished to go a little higher up to the southwest from the foot of the hill. They then measured off another one hundred varas in the same direction. I told them I wished to locate my lot somewhere in that limit from the beach. The magistrate Don Francisco de Haro told me in the presence of the ayuntamiento that he must have a starting point from the southeast so that he could fix the lot. He then appointed the first sand hill to the southeast from where we were standing as the southeast boundary. He then went to that first sand hill with the ayuntamiento and I accompanied them, and he pointed the direction in which the street must lay. He then told me that I could take the first one hundred vara lot from the starting point, or any other one hundred vara lot in the direction to the northwest. He commenced measuring and measured off the first three one hundred vara lots, and on measuring the fourth one, I wished to take one half of the fourth and one half of the fifth lot, as these parts were just where it came on the cleared part of the plain and left it more open. He told me he could not give me a half lot but I might take any one complete one hundred vara lot any where in that direction. I selected the fifth one hundred vara lot from the starting point. He measured off no more in that direction, but declared all the land in that direction in that line to the waters of the bay as the northwest boundary for the small settlement of the Yerba Buena, and at the same time laid off the street in that same direction which he called Calle de la Fundacion [Foundation Street], and measured two hundred varas more from the southwest side of my lot to the southwest running into the hills which he called the southwest boundary, being parallel to the street above named of the small village of Yerba Buena. The southeast limits were three hundred varas from said street in a southwest direction from the commencement of the street and from that same street in a northeast direction along the sand hill into the bay—the borders of the water from that point all around towards the northwest to what is now called the North Beach, at the point where the southwest boundary came to the bay, formed the other boundary. The first two hundred varas measured off on the beach were reserved for Government purposes.

The first sand hill [forming the limit of Yerba Buena on the southeast] was between the streets now called California St. and Pine St. and it was nearest to Pine St.

The starting point [of the Calle de la Fundacion] is near the present corner of Pine and Kearny Sts., but not quite so far south as Pine St.

Jacob P. Leese was the first settler who came after me. He came and built his house on the third of July 1836. His lot was adjoining that lot that I had possession of to the southeast.

Plan of Yerba Buena, 1839.

Tracing of a diseño (a land-grant map), probably by Jacob P. Leese, when he and Salvador Vallejo applied for two one-hundred vara lots at Yerba Buena's embarcadero (at the foot of present-day Broadway), for the purpose of erecting buildings and a wharf. (The lettering has been copied, not traced.) Leese was the town's second resident, having arrived in 1836.

The Calle de la Fundacion is shown, but not named, and Richardson's house is shown. Other named features are the road to the mission, Rincon Point, the lake at the foot of where Sacramento Street will be, the Embarcadero and the Leese and Vallejo building lot, the plot owned by Castañares, and the Beach of Juana Briones. Telegraph Hill and the trail to the presidio are shown but not named.

Yerba Buena in the Spring of 1837
from a lithograph of a watercolor painting by Jean Jacques Vioget.

At the left is the trading schooner of Jacob P. Leese. The houses of Richardson and Leese, the only two structures in Yerba Buena at the time, are directly above the prow of the ship's boat.

Jean Jacques Vioget (1799–1855), a Swiss-born soldier, sailor, and surveyor, came to San Francisco in 1837 as the master of an Ecuadorian brig, the *Delmira,* and traded along the California coast for the next two years.

He was also an artist, as can be seen by the illustration on the preceding page, and spoke several languages. And he also seemed to have been a *bon vivant,* good at the basic talents and attributes that make a man well liked by his fellow men—that is, good at eating and drinking, and good at repartee and enjoying a good laugh. Partly for these reasons, and partly because he was a property owner in the town and the only man on the spot with the requisite talents, in 1839 he was chosen by the alcalde, Francisco Guerrero, to make the first official survey of the town of Yerba Buena.

Vioget produced a strange survey: the streets were not at right angles, but rather were off by 2½°. Why do it that way? The question has never been answered. The only reasonable explanation is that Vioget was taking into account the locations of the existing structures, which had been erected without regard to a street system. Nevertheless, it was something that would have to be fixed, sooner or later.

Vioget's survey of Yerba Buena in 1839 showed the owned property at the time, the limits of the village, the original *Calle de la Fundacion,* (which would not appear on future maps), and the lagoons, which would soon disappear, near where the waterfront was then. The survey covered the area from Montgomery to Stockton streets and from California to Pacific streets, although none of the streets had as yet been named.

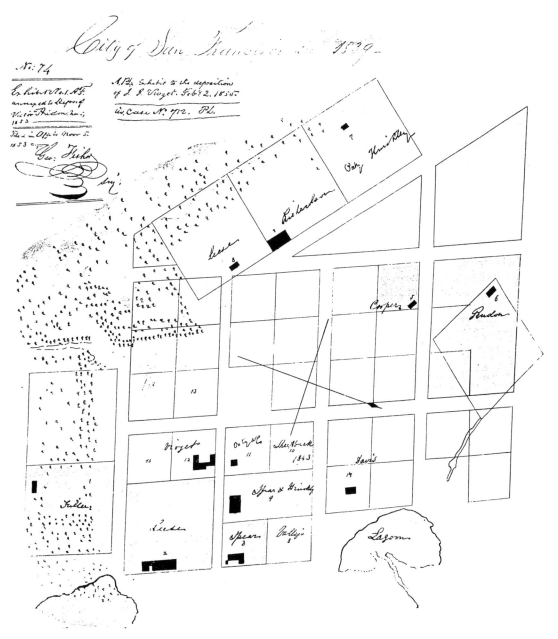

Vioget's Plan of Yerba Buena, 1839.

William D. Phelps was engaged in the hide and tallow trade on
the Pacific coast from 1840 to 1846. These excerpts from his book
Fore and Aft recount his experiences when he was at San Francisco
Bay in July and August of 1841.

He was proud to have taken a ship's boat farther up the Sacramento than anyone before him. He also supplies an unusual
glimpse of what social life amounted to in the village of Yerba
Buena.

William D. Phelps

From:

Fore and Aft; or, Leaves From the Life of an Old Sailor

In 1841, Yerba Buena was in an almost uninhabitable condition. In the early part of that year there were but four permanent residents there,—J. V. Leese, Nathan Spear, John Davis, and Jack Fuller. Seated on the top of Telegraph Hill, with the whole expanse of the broad bay spread before him, one might look in the direction from Sansitio [Sausalito] to Angel Island, across the Bay of San Pablo to the Contra Coast, and away south towards San Jose and Santa Clara, without seeing a single sail of ship, boat, or any other craft moving over its waters,—the only signs of humanity being confined to the few dwellers at the cove. Perhaps, on another day, from the same place of observation, might be seen a solitary ship at anchor, seeking for hides; or above Angel Island an old launch at anchor, two days out from Yerba Buena, bound to Sansitio, where lived Captain Richardson, the Port Captain of a port then without ships, but where it was hoped they might come hereafter. He was also the owner of all the navigation belonging in the bay, consisting of two old launches. Perhaps once a month he would cross the bay in one of them, rigged with a temporary mast and piece of old canvas for a sail, the crew consisting of himself and two Indians. Dropping down with the last ebb, he calculated on taking the flood tide in the vicinity of Alcatras Island, and, as it swept him far up the bay, he would endeavor to make northing enough to get through Angel Island Straits when a favorable opportunity offered, which he would wait for at anchor.

As showing the condition of the region round about the cove, I may also state that Mr. Leese came on board the ship one morning to breakfast, and told us that the evening previous an Indian boy, eight years old, was taken away from his yard by a panther, which had been seen prowling around the settlement for some days previous. Mr. Leese's house stood where the corner of Dupont and Clay Streets now is. The boy was not seen afterwards. Again, during the same year, the second officer, with a gang of men, was sent on shore from my ship to cut firewood on Rincon Point. At noon they went towards a tree where they had left a firkin containing their dinner, and found a she "grizzly" and her cub, with the firkin between them, discussing its contents. The wooding party made for the shore as fast as possible, and hailed to be taken off. This was repeated a few days after, when, with a party well armed, we went on shore to hunt the beasts. We tracked the creatures to where they took the water at Mission Creek, and heard no more of them.

Up to July 27th of the same year, the river Sacramento had never been ascended by a ship's boat. The Bay of San Francisco was well surveyed by Beechy [sic], but no survey was known to have been made of the waters above the Bay of San Pablo. On the day of the above date, I left the ship with the cutter and six men, well armed and equipped, for the purpose of visiting Captain Sutter, who had begun a settlement about a hundred miles above the bay. I had previously formed an acquaintance with this gentleman, and, from his glowing account of the beauty of the country in that region, and his assurance that a keel boat had not disturbed the waters of the Rio El Sacramento, I felt very desirous to be the first visitor there from the sea. For three months previous, the Captain and supercargoes of the two ships who were to anchor at the bay, and to whom I proposed the expedition, were very eager to join in it, but when the time came to move in the matter, they could not go, and made many excuses. "It was a bad season of the year, the river was low and the weather hot, mosquitoes ravenous, bears were numerous, and the Indians cannibals." I had made my preparations, and I went without them. The remarks that follow are extracts taken from my log-book which I kept at the time.

Leaving the ship at noon, we crossed the passage with a strong breeze in our favor. We passed through the Bay of San Pablo, the Straits of Carquines, and ran across the Bay of Sia Suni [Suisun]. We entered the Sacramento just after sundown, passing the outlet of the San Joaquin about a mile inside of the mouth of the Sacramento. . . . There was water enough for a frigate to pass through the Straits, but there were shoal spots between that and the river. With a strong, fair wind, and a bright moon, we kept on until the low "Tule," or flag bottoms, were passed; reaching the high wooded banks, we encamped for the night under a large sycamore, where we built a fire and made coffee. After a hearty supper we spread our blankets, and, regardless of who might be our neighbors, slept soundly until daylight. After breakfast we started again. The camp we left I judged to be about ninety-five miles from the ship. We had scarcely pushed off from the bank when we observed a good-sized panther smelling around the spot where we had breakfasted. I gave him a parting shot, when he moved off, perhaps hit, perhaps not. The greater part of this day was passed in sailing and rowing against a strong tide; the heat was so intense that we had to stop occasionally under the wide-spreading shade of some lofty sycamore. . . . The next day, at 11 A.M., we arrived at a rancherie [sic] of Indians belonging to a tribe under the jurisdiction of Captain Sutter. There were about thirty of them stationed here, to catch and cure fish for the Captain's establishment. The place was afterwards called the "Russian Embarcadero"; it was about fifteen miles from Sutter's by the river, but less than half that distance by land.

The heat being quite oppressive, I concluded to rest here in the shade, and send a note across to Captain Sutter, requesting that a horse be sent to me. One of the Indians understood a little Spanish, and I had no trouble in making my wishes understood by the old chief, who sent one of his fleet runners with my note. In about three hours the Major-domo of Captain Sutter arrived, bringing a fine saddle-horse for me, and I rode with my guide over a beautiful and rich tract of country, abounding with flowers, shrubbery, and forest. Coming in sight of the fort, I was unexpectedly received by a military salute of cannon, and a gay display of flags. I received a most cordial welcome, and was soon seated at dinner, which consisted mostly of venison cooked in various ways. . . .

About three miles from Sutter's Fort, on the right bank of the American Fork, resided John Sinclair, who planted himself here shortly after Captain Sutter made a beginning. Sinclair was an intelligent Scotchman of considerable education, hardy and enterprising; he had been some years in the employ of the Hudson [sic] Bay Company, but possessed too much spirit and independence to remain subject to the arbitrary requirements of that service. He left it and went to the Sandwich Islands, and for some time edited a newspaper there, but his old habits of hunting and trapping were too strong to be overcome, and he emigrated to California. In connection with his neighbor, Captain Sutter, he managed to control a number of Indian tribes, among whom they found abundant help in cultivating their wheat-fields and managing cattle. These two men, at the time of my first visit, were the only ones in that region who had "a habitation and a name."

I spent a week in exploring the river above New Helvetia, as the settlement was called, enjoyed a successful elk hunt with my host, and returned down the river much gratified with my visit. My good friends, Captain Sutter and Mr. Sinclair, had collected a great many beautiful articles of Indian manufacture, such as fine woven ornamental baskets, feather blankets, bows, arrows, etc., which they kindly forced me to accept; as I was their first visitor from the sea, they said I was entitled to them.

Dropping down the river at night, with a bright moon and a cloudless sky, the scene was indeed lovely. It was quite calm; I let the rowers lay on their oars, to take a nap, while the current was sweeping us along. The river at this place was broad; on either side were spread thick primeval forests, where the sound of the axe had never been heard; the lofty sycamores threw their broad shade along the margin of the silver surface of the beautiful river; but all was silent, save the chirping of the cricket, and the gentle rippling of the eddies as the majestic torrent moved in solitary grandeur to mingle with the sea. I saw the waters run and shoot onward like the course of destiny, and I thought how the tide of time sweeps on to eternity. So passes man! How applicable are the lines of Byron to this solitude. He sang of its sister river, "Where rolls the Oregon, and hears no sound save his own dashings." Here the waters are seldom disturbed by the oar or whitened by a sail; the trapper paddles his canoe along the margin to entrap the beaver, or, monthly, a sail-boat from New Helvetia drops down on her way to Yerba Buena; all else is silent. We reached the ship on the third day.

Hudson's Bay Company

In January 1842 the Company's bark *Cowlitz* came to San Francisco with a cargo of goods, to open a general traffic with the people of the country, and, in short, to monopolize the trade of California. With the ship came Sir George Simpson, the Deputy Governor of the Company, and Doctor McLaughlin, the chief factor, together with a number of under officers of various grades. The house built by Jacob P. Leese, with a hundred vara lot of land, was purchased, their cargo landed, and their first trading-post in California was then established.

When the ship left the port, Mr. Glen Rae, an under factor, and son-in-law of Dr. McLaughlin [McLoughlin], was left in charge of the business. Mt. Rae was a Scotchman (as most of the Company's officers were), and very socially inclined. We Yankees were desirous of finding out the intentions of our powerful competitors, and were often visitors at the establishment of our friend Rae, especially at evening, when he was prone to indulge in the "barley brae." At such times he was quite communicative. In one of his merry moods he told us that it cost his Company seventy-five thousand pounds to drive Bryant & Sturgis from the North-west fur trade. "And they will drive you Yankees," he said, "from California, if it costs a million."

Before leaving here, Sir George and other of the Company's officers proceeded down the coast. He had lately crossed from the Atlantic, via Hudson Bay, to the Columbia River, partly in canoes, visiting all the principal stations and trading-posts on the route from the Columbia to their extreme northern post, touching the Russian territory, thence to the Sandwich Islands. And now in California he was visiting every part of the coast, spying out all business that was doing, and who was doing it, making himself acquainted with the people, dancing at their fandangoes with the pretty Senoritas, and their mothers also, puffing a cigaritto with the old Don, and sparing no effort or expense to make a good impression for the interests of the great Company he represented. Sir George, in fact, was a man of indomitable energy and perseverance, of free and courteous manners, and a great favorite with all; but he could not compete with the Boston traders. Their system of doing business was different, and far better adapted to the condition of the Californians.

At the time of this visit the Company had a trading party of seventy men above the Bay of San Francisco, in charge of Mr. Ermitinger [sic], who was Captain of all the Company's hunters and trappers west of the mountains.[1] I met this gentleman frequently while visiting his friend Rae, at the Yerba Buena, and was much interested in him. He was a fair specimen of many who have risen to positions of responsibility by long and laborious service. Beginning at the lowest round of the ladder, with low pay, compelled to perform duty in any capacity and in any place to which they may be ordered, at the desk, or chopping wood, pulling an oar or cultivating the ground, the Company's servants are promoted, from time to time, according to their capacity and merit. Ermitinger was a good representative man of his class,—hardy, vigorous, and active; extravagant in word, thought, and deed, heedless of hardship, daring of danger, prodigal of the present, and thoughtless of the future. Twenty-five years' life as a trapper and a chief of trappers, had accustomed him to perilous encounters with bears and Indians. His simple and frank manner in relating them contrasted singularly with the wild and startling nature of his themes. I was amused at a remark of his, which showed the contempt in which these sons of the wilderness hold the comforts of civilized life. "Captain," said he, "this is the first time I have slept in a house for two years, and last night I did a thing which I have not done for twenty-four years: I slept in sheets,

---

1. Francis Ermatinger (1798–1858) was born in Portugal and educated in England. He joined the Hudson's Bay Company in 1818, and remained in the employ of the Company until 1853. According to the *Encyclopedia of Frontier Biography*, "He was generally liked and respected, if sometimes impetuous and occasionally harsh."

but I was drunk, and Rae put me into them, therefore the sin must lie at his door."

One evening I was at Mr. Rae's, at a small party. Ermitinger was present. In the course of the evening Padre ——, of the Mission of Saint Rafael, entered the room, pretty well "sprung," and began to use disgusting familiarities with the company, such as hugging and kissing the gentlemen after the Spanish fashion,—which is annoying to most people, especially when the parties are both of the male sex. The priest embraced those he knew, and proposed to extend his fraternal caress to Ermitinger, who was a stranger. After an introduction, when he made advances for that purpose, the trapper tried to avoid the contact. He told him "he was glad to see him, but he did not allow any man to put his hands on him." In vain we tried to keep the priest quiet; but as he increased his libations, so grew his foolish persistence. Making a desperate effort to accomplish his purpose, most unexpectedly he came in contact with the back of the hunter's hand, which sent him sprawling across the room. "Stranger," said Ermitinger, "when I was in the Rocky Mountains I swore that I would never allow myself to be hugged by a Blackfoot Indian or a grizzly bear; but I would suffer the embraces of either in preference to those of a drunken priest." The poor Padre found he was "barking up the wrong tree;" and as his cowl and shaven crown found but little reverence in such rude company, he thought he had better leave, which he accordingly did.

The advent of the Mormons

The ship *Brooklyn*, of and from New York, arrived at Yerba Buena August 2d, with about fifty Mormon families. I called on board to look at them; they appeared to be of the middling class, mostly stout men, mechanics and farmers. Their Elder, who, by the way, was not elderly looking, but young and dandyish in appearance (Mr. S. Brannon) [sic] handed me a Sandwich Island newspaper (they had called at Honolulu), containing an account which he had furnished the editor, stating their views, and the object which led them to California. They were the pioneers of a large body of their sect who were on their way to possess this land, which a revelation from heaven had shown them they must occupy, and here they must establish a new republic of their own, extend the dominion of the Saints on the shores of the Pacific, and eventually over India and China. They were sadly disappointed to find the flag of the United States waving here, and that, regardless of their divine right, their "Uncle Samuel" had possession of the promised land.

The Mormons were prepared to take forcible measures if they found it necessary for this purpose; they were well armed, and had improved their time during the long passage in infantry drill and the use of the musket; they had a flag of their own, but as it was not unfurled in California I cannot describe it.

Their arrival, and their own statements of their intentions in taking what they pleased from the people without their leave, caused some excitement at first; but as they did not actually molest any person or property, and soon settled down to various employments, were industrious and well behaved, there was nothing to distinguish them from other emigrants. Their leader turned his attention to more profitable pursuits, and became one of the most energetic and successful citizens in the country.

Sir George Simpson, the Governor of the Hudson's Bay Company, arrived at San Francisco Bay at the end of December 1841—another stop on an around-the-world journey in which he traveled mainly by ship, but crossed Canada from Montreal to Vancouver by canoe and on foot. His specific purpose at San Francisco Bay was to check on the functioning of an HBC store that had been established at Yerba Buena in the fall of 1841 by William Glen Rae, the son-in-law of Chief Factor John McLoughlin at Fort Vancouver.

The HBC had the intention of capturing the fur trade on the California coast, as it had done throughout much of Canada. But these hopes never were realized, because of intense American competition and because Sir George Simpson, for one, quite clearly anticipated the coming American tide, and the inability of England or anyone else to stop it.

Sir George Simpson

From:

An Overland Journey Round the World, during the Years 1841 and 1842.

On the morning of the thirtieth, a light breeze enabled us again to get under way and to work into the port. After crossing a bar, on which, however, there is a sufficient depth of water, we entered a strait of about two miles in width—just narrow enough for the purposes of military defence—observing, on the southern side of the mouth, a fort well situated for commanding the passage, but itself commanded by a hill behind. This fort is now dismantled and dilapidated; nor are its remains likely to last long, for the soft rock, on the very verge of which they already hang, is fast crumbling into the undermining tide beneath. A short distance beyond the fort, and on the same side of the strait, is situated a square of huts, distinguished by the lofty title of the Presidio of San Francisco, and tenanted, for garrisoned it is not, by a commandant and as many soldiers as might, if all told, muster the rank and file of a corporal's party; and, though here the softness of the rock does nothing to aid the national alacrity in decaying, yet the adobes or unbaked bricks, of which Captain Prado's strong hold is composed, have already succeeded in rendering this establishment as much of a ruin as the other.

On proceeding along the strait, one of the most attractive scenes imaginable gradually opens on the mariner's view,—a sheet of water of about thirty miles in length by about twelve in breadth, sheltered from every wind by an amphitheatre of green hills, while an intermediate belt of open plain, varying from two to six miles in depth, is dotted by the habitations of civilized men.

On emerging from the strait, which is about three miles long, we saw on our left in a deep bay, known as Whaler's Harbor, two vessels, the government schooner California and the Russian brig Constantine, now bound to Sitka with the last of the tenants of Bodega and Ross on board. As we observed the Russians getting under way, I dispatched Mr. Hopkins in one of our boats to express my regret at being thus deprived of the anticipated pleasure of paying my respects in person. Mr. Hopkins found about a hundred souls, men, women and children, all patriotically delighted to exchange the lovely climate of California for the ungenial skies of Sitka, and that, too, at the expense of making a long voyage in an old, crazy, clumsy tub, at the stormiest season of the year; but to this general rule there had been one exception, inasmuch as they had lost two days in waiting, but alas in vain, for a young woman, who had abjured alike her country and her husband for the sake of one of the dons of San Francisco.

Mr. Hopkins farther learned that, though it was Thursday with us, yet it was Friday with our northern friends,—a circumstance which, besides showing us that the Russians had not the superstition of our tars as to days of sailing, forcibly reminded us that between them the two parties had passed round the globe in opposite directions to prosecute one and the same trade in furs, which the indolent inhabitants of the province were too lazy to appropriate at their very doors.

On our right, just opposite to the ground occupied by the Constantine and the California, stretched the pretty little bay of Yerba Buena, whose shores are doubtless destined, under better auspices, to be the site of a flourishing town, though at present they contain only eight or nine houses in addition to The Hudson's Bay Company's establishment. Here we dropped anchor in the neighborhood of four other vessels, the American barque Alert and brig Bolivar, the British barque Index and the Mexican brig Catilina, and, after firing a salute, went ashore to visit Mr. Rae, the Hudson's Bay Company's representative in this quarter.

Bay of San Francisco

The sheet of water, as already described, forms only a part of the inland sea of San Francisco. Whaler's Harbor, at its own northern extremity, communicates by a strait of about two miles in width, with the Bay of San Pedro [San Pablo Bay], a circular basin of ten miles in diameter; and again this extensive pool, at its northeastern end, leads by means of a second strait into Freshwater Bay of nearly the same form and magnitude, which is full of islands, and forms the receptacle of the Sacramento and the San Joachin. Large vessels, it is said, may penetrate into Freshwater Bay; and as the San Joachin and the Sacramento, which drain vast tracts of country respectively to the southeast and to the northeast, are navigable for inland craft, the whole harbor, besides its matchless qualities as a port of refuge on this surf-beaten coast, is the outlet of a vast breadth of fair and fertile land.

In the face of all these advantages and temptations, the good folks of San Francisco, priests as well as laymen, and laymen as well as priests, have been contented to borrow, for their aquatic excursions, the native balsa,—a kind of raft or basket which, when wanted, can be constructed in a few minutes with the bulrushes that spring so luxuriantly on the margins of the lakes and rivers. In this miserable makeshift they contrive to cross the inland waters, and perhaps, in very choice weather, to venture a little way out to sea,—there being, I believe, no other floating thing besides, neither boat nor canoe, neither barge nor scow, in any part of the harbor, or, in fact, in any part of Upper California, from San Diego on the south to San Francisco on the north. In consequence of this state of things, the people of the bay have been so far from availing themselves of their internal channels of communication, that their numerous expeditions into the interior have all been conducted by land, seldom leading, of course, to any result commensurate with the delay and expense. But, inconvenient as the entire want of small craft must be to the dwellers on such an inlet as has been described, there are circumstances which do, to a certain extent, account for the protracted endurance of the evil. Horses are almost as plentiful as bulrushes; time is a perfect glut with a community of loungers; and, under the plea of having no means of catching fish, the faithful enjoy, by a standing dispensation, the comfortable privilege of fasting at meagre times on their hecatombs of beef.

The trade of the bay, and, in fact, of the whole province, is entirely in the hands of foreigners, who are almost exclusively of the English race. Of that race, however, the Americans are considerably more numerous than the British,—the former naturally flocking in greater force to neutral ground, such as this country and the Sandwich Islands, while the latter find a variety of advantageous outlets in their own national colonies. At present the foreigners are to the Californians in number as one to ten, being about 600 out of about 7,000, while, by their monopoly of trade and their command of resources, to say nothing of their superior energy and intelligence, they already possess vastly more than their numerical proportion of political influence; and their position in this respect excites the less jealousy, inasmuch as most of them have been induced, either by a desire of shaking off legal incapacities or by less interested motives, to profess the Catholic religion and to marry into provincial families.

The Californians of San Francisco number between 2,000 and 2,500, about 700 belonging to the village or *pueblo* of San Jose de Guadalupe and the remainder occupying about thirty farms of various sizes, generally subdivided among the families of the respective holders.

On the score of industry, these good folks, as also their brethren of the

other ports, are perhaps the least promising colonists of a new country in
the world, being, in this respect, decidedly inferior to what the savages
themselves had become under the training of the priests; so that the
spoliation of the missions, excepting that it has opened the province to
general enterprise, has directly tended to nip civilization in the bud. In the
missions there were large flocks of sheep; but now there are scarcely any
left, The Hudson's Bay Company having, last spring, experienced great
difficulty in collecting about four thousand for its northern settlements.

In the missions the wool used to be manufactured into coarse cloth; and
it is, in fact, because the Californians are too lazy to weave or spin,—too
lazy, I suspect, even to clip and wash the raw material,—that the sheep
have been literally destroyed to make more room for the horned cattle.
In the missions, soap and leather used to be made; but in such vulgar
processes the Californians advance no farther than nature herself has
advanced before them, excepting to put each animal's tallow in one place
and its hide in another. In the missions the dairy formed a principal object
of attention; but now neither butter nor cheese nor any preparation of milk
whatever is to be found in the province. In the missions there were annually produced about eighty thousand bushels of wheat and maize, the
former, and perhaps part of the latter also, being converted into flour; but
the present possessors of the soil do so little in the way of tilling the
ground, that, when lying at Monterey, we sold to the government some
barrels of flour at the famine-rate of twenty-eight dollars, or nearly six
pounds sterling a sack,—a price which could not be considered as merely
local, for the stuff was intended to victual the same schooner which, on our
first arrival, we had seen at anchor in Whaler's Harbor. In the missions,
beef was occasionally cured for exportation; but so miserably is the case
now reversed, that, though meat enough to supply the fleets of England
is annually either consumed by fire or left to the carrion-birds, yet the
authorities purchased from us, along with the flour just mentioned, some
salted salmon as indispensable sea-stores for the one paltry vessel, which
constituted the entire line-of-battle of the Californian navy. In the missions
a great deal of wine was grown, good enough to be sent for sale to Mexico;
but, with the exception of what we got at the Mission of Santa Barbara, the
native wine, that we tasted, was such trash as nothing but politeness could
have induced us to swallow.

Various circumstances have conspired to render these dons so very
peculiarly indolent. Independently of innate differences of national tastes,
the objects of colonization exert an influence over the character of the
colonists. Thus the energy of our republican brethren and the prosperity of
the contiguous dependencies of the empire are to be traced, in a great

degree, to the original and permanent necessity of relying on the steady and laborious use of the axe and the plough; and thus also the rival colonists of New France,—a name which comprehended the valleys of the St. Lawrence and the Mississippi,—dwindled and pined on much of the same ground, partly because the golden dreams of the fur-trade carried them away from stationary pursuits to overrun half the breadth of the continent, and partly because the gigantic ambition of their government regarded them rather as soldiers than as settlers, rather as the instruments of political aggrandizement than as the germ of a kindred people. In like manner, Spanish America, with its sierras of silver, became the asylum and paradise of idlers, holding out to every adventurer, when leaving the shores of the old country, the prospect of earning his bread without the sweat of his brow.

But the population of California in particular has been drawn from the most indolent variety of an indolent species, being composed of superannuated troopers and retired office holders and their descendants. In connection with the establishment of the missions, at least of those of the upper province, there had been projected three villages or pueblos, as place of refuge for such of the old soldiers as might obtain leave to settle in the country; but, as the priests were by no means friendly to the rise of a separate interest, they did all in their power to prevent the requisite licenses from being granted by the crown, so as to send to the villages as few denizens as possible, and to send them only when they were past labor as well in ability as in inclination. These villages were occasionally strengthened by congenial reinforcements of runaway sailors, and, in order to avoid such sinks of profligacy and riot, the better sort of functionaries, both civil and military, gradually established themselves elsewhere, but more particularly at Santa Barbara, while both classes were frequently coming into collision with the fathers, whose vexatious spirit of exclusiveness, even after the emancipation of the veterans, often prompted them nominally to pre-occupy lands which they did not require. Such settlers of either class were not likely to toil for much more than what the cheap bounty of nature afforded them, horses to ride and beef to eat, with hides and tallow to exchange for such other supplies as they wanted. In a word, they displayed more than the proverbial indolence of a pastoral people, for they did not even devote their idle hours to the tending of their herds.

As one might have expected, the children improved on the example of the parents through the influence of a systematic education,—an education which gave them the lasso as a toy in infancy and the horse as a companion in boyhood, which, in short, trained them from the cradle to be mounted bullock-hunters, and nothing else; and, if anything could aggravate their laziness, it was the circumstance that many of them dropped, as it were, into ready-made competency by sharing in the lands and cattle of the plundered missions. . . .

The Americans only want a rallying point for carrying into effect their theory, that the English race is destined by "right divine" to expel the Spaniards from their ancient seats—a theory which has already begun to develop itself in more ways than one. American adventurers have repeatedly stolen cattle and horses by wholesale, with as little compunction as if they had merely helped themselves to an installment of their own property. American trappers have frequently stalked into the Californian towns with their long rifles ready for all sorts of mischief, practically setting the government at defiance, and putting the inhabitants in bodily fear. . . .

The Americans, if masters of the interior, will soon discover that they have a natural right to a maritime outlet; so that, whatever may be the fate of Monterey, and the more southerly ports, San Francisco will, to a moral certainty, sooner or later fall into the possession of Americans; the only possible mode of preventing such a result, being the previous occupation of the port on the part of Great Britain. English, in some sense or other of the word, the richest portions of California must become—either Great Britain will introduce her well regulated freedom of all classes and colors, or the people of the United States will inundate the country with their own peculiar mixture of helpless bondage and lawless insubordination. Between two such alternatives the Californians themselves have little room for choice; and, even if there were ground for hesitation, they would, I am convinced, find in their actual experience sufficient reason for deciding in favor of the British, for they specially and emphatically complain that the Americans, in their mercantile dealings, are too wide awake for such drowsy customers as would rather be cheated at once than protect themselves by any unusual expenditure of vigilance and caution. . . .

On our return to Yerba Buena, we made arrangements with Don Francisco Guerrero . . . for visiting him at the mission of San Francisco, the oldest establishment of the kind on the bay and the nearest to our anchorage. On the morning of Monday, the tenth of the month, Guerrero's horses were in attendance; and a pleasant ride of three miles over some sandy hills, covered with the dwarf oak and the strawberry tree, brought us to the mission of San Francisco. In the case of San Francisco Solano [at Sonoma], the remains of the original establishment had been replaced or eclipsed by the more ambitious buildings of General Vallego [sic]; but here one wilderness of ruins presented nothing to blend the promise of the future with the story of the past. This scene of desolation had not even the charm of antiquity to grace it, for, as it was only in 1776 that the mission was founded, the oldest edifice, that now crumbled before us, had not equaled the span of human life, the age of three-score years and ten; and yet, when compared with the stubborn piles which elsewhere perish so gradually as to exhibit no perceptible change to a single generation of men, these ruins had attained a state of decay which would have done credit to the wind and weather of centuries. Oddly enough the endemic laziness of the country had, in this instance, run ahead of Old Time with his jog-trot and his scythe, and had done his work for him at a smarter pace and with more formidable tools. In plain English, the indolent Californians had saved themselves a vast deal of woodsman's and carpenter's labor by carrying off doors and windows and roofs, leaving the unsheltered adobes, if one may name small things with great, to the fate of Nineveh and Babylon. But these good Catholics did set a limit, and that, too, a characteristic one, to their sacrilege. They could appropriate the cattle, and dismantle the dwellings of the missions, robbing both priests and proselytes of what they had earned in common by the sweat of their brows; but they respected the churches with a superstitious awe, even after they had degraded them into baubles by the expulsion at once of the pastors and their flocks. They left the mint and the anise and the cumin untouched, but trampled on the weightier matters of the law; they reverenced the altar but disclaimed the mercy of which it was the emblem. Of this hollow show, however, the friars should partly bear the blame. It was an external religion that they had taught: they had sown the wind and were reaping the whirlwind.

In former days there resided here, besides the priests and soldiers, about seven hundred domesticated converts, of whom we saw only three naked, dirty, miserable creatures. In 1776, the mission had commenced operations with five cattle, the ancestors of the thousand herds that now crowd the shores of the bay; but, towards the close of its career, it had acquired about fifteen thousand descendants of the original stock for its own single share, besides considerable flocks of sheep and large bands of horses. When times of trouble, however, arrived, the priests, as I have already stated in a general way, so successfully forestalled the spoilers by killing off their animals, that the first administrador of the mission of San Francisco came into possession of not more than five thousand cattle; and this number has since been reduced to about three hundred, that are now running wild on the hills.

Priests, cattle, savages and dwellings had all vanished. Nor were the spiritual results of the system more conspicuous than its material fruits, consisting, as they did, of nothing but a negative veneration for the ornaments and appendages of a deserted place of worship.

But the mission, though dead, still spake through its interesting associations. As I had perused, during our tedious voyage in the *Cowlitz*, Forbes's History of California, with its many curious details in the shape of the authentic records of the establishments, every object in the present solitude, not even excepting the mouldering adobe, had its own tale to tell of the motley life of bygone days. In making the tour of the ruins, we first entered the apartment in which the priests took their meals and received visits,—two branches of business which they understood to perfection. To say nothing of the grand staples of beef and frixoles, their tables groaned under a profusion of mutton, fowls, vegetables, fruits, bread, pastry, milk, butter and cheese, of everything, in short, which a prolific soil and an almost tropical climate could be made to yield to industry and art; and as their dining-room was connected with their kitchen by a small closet, which served merely to intercept the grosser perfumes, they had evidently known, contrary to modern use and wont, how to heighten the zest of these good things by attacking them hot and racy from the fire, and cooling them, if necessary, for themselves with the juice of their own grapes. These were the times for traveling in California. Besides its agreeable society and its hospitable board, every mission was more ready than its neighbor to supply the visitor with guides, and horses and provisions, whether for visiting the immediate neighborhood, or for prosecuting his journey through the province; and, if one did not look too critically below the surface, the contrast between the untamed savages and the half-civilized converts could hardly fail to complete, in the eyes of the hasty wayfarer, a kind of terrestrial paradise.

Passing through the dining-room, we were conducted into a square surrounded with buildings, in which, to say nothing of less important avocations, the natives used to be employed in manufacturing the wool of the establishment into blankets and coarse cloths, their wheels and looms having been made by themselves under the direction of their zealous teachers, who had derived their knowledge on the subject from books. It was, in fact, chiefly by means of books that the missionaries had contrived to overcome all the difficulties of their isolated position, from the preparing of the adobes to the decorating of the churches, from the constructing of the plough to the baking of the bread, from the shearing of the sheep to the fulling of the web. But, in addition to their ingenuity in planning, they toiled more diligently than any of their unwilling assistants in the actual execution of their various labors, striving at the same time to render their drudgery morally available as an example. Thus, for instance, did the astute and indefatigable fathers temper the mud with measured steps and merry ditties in order to beguile, if possible, their indolent and simple pupils into useful labor by the attractions of the song and the dance. The praise of all this, however, should, in a great degree, be awarded to the Jesuits, who, before they were supplanted by the Franciscans, had covered the sterile rocks of Lower California with the monuments, agricultural and architectural, and economical, of their patience and aptitude, not only leaving to their successors apposite models and tolerable workmen, but also bequeathing to them the invaluable lesson that nothing was impossible to energy and perseverance. Still the system, in spite of all the sacrifices of the two foremost orders of the Romish Church, was but a show, in which the puppets ceased to dance when the wire-pullers were withdrawn; it was a body without a soul of its own, which could move only by the infusion of extraneous life; it was, in a word, typified by its own adobe, which nothing but constant care and attention could prevent from returning to its elementary dust.

From the factory we went to the church. This was a large edifice, almost as plain as a barn excepting in front, where it was prettily finished with small columns, on which was hung a peal of bells. The interior, however, of the building presented a prodigality of ornament. The ceiling was painted all over; the walls were covered with pictures and pieces of sculpture; and the altar displayed all the appointments of the Romish service in a style, which, for this country, might well be characterized as gorgeous. Even to our Protestant tastes the general effect was considerably heightened by the "dim religious light" of two or three narrow windows, which themselves appeared to be buried in the recesses of a wall between five and six feet thick. The church, as I have already said, remained in perfect preservation amidst the contrast of the surrounding ruins; and considering the solidity of the walls, which, to say nothing of their thickness, had become vitrified by time, it could hardly be destroyed in any other way than by the removal of its roof.

In the vicinity of the church was formerly situated the garden, which, being within the ordinary range of the northwest fogs, had always been inferior to the gardens of the more inland missions. It was now choked with weeds and bushes; and the walls were broken down in many places, though, by a characteristic exertion of Californian industry, piles of skulls had filled up some of the gaps, reminding one of the pound of buffalo-bones, a hundred feet square and five or six feet high, which had been constructed, a year or two ago, by the Indians of the prairies on the eastern side of the mountains. . . .

We felt highly gratified by our visit, the more so as the day was bright and warm; and, after paying our respects to Senora Guerrero, a pretty young woman with black eyes and white teeth, we returned to Yerba Buena on the alcalde's steeds.

This reminiscent view of Yerba Buena appeared in the *Sacramento Daily Union* on August 26 and September 16, 1871. The writer was Edward Cleveland Kemble, who, although not a Mormon, had arrived at Yerba Buena on July 31, 1846 with Sam Brannan's contingent of Mormon immigrants on the *Brooklyn*.

Kemble had worked with Brannan on the latter's New York newspaper, and in Yerba Buena/San Francisco he continued under Brannan as editor of *The California Star*. Later he bought the *Star*, merged it with *The Californian*, and published the merged papers for five weeks in late 1848. On January 4, 1849, Kemble and two others began publication of the long-lived *Alta California*.

Yerba Buena—1846

A Backward Look
The *Sacramento Daily Union*, August 26, 1871

My certificate of membership in the San Francisco "Pioneers," framed and hanging against the wall, is a spirited cluster of sketches by Nahl,[1] illustrating California life and scenery, the views represented by openings through the vines and branches of what may be a mammoth tree on the one side and the famous grape vine of Santa Barbara on the other. There are eight of these little scenes surrounding the shield which bears the record of membership. Those in the two lower corners of the engraving are beheld from under spreading branches and between rolling mists, and are views of some historical pretension. They furnish an outlook from my present home and "roof-tree," thousands of miles away, back through the mists of years to some of the wild scenes of boyhood. Through the loopholes in my wall, I look twenty-five years back into the past of California.

One of the views through these openings is a somewhat distorted sketch of the site of San Francisco when it was known as the "cove and anchorage of Yerba Buena." The other looks off in the pathway of the setting sun, through the entrance of the bay and out through the Golden Gate. The view in both cases is from the hills in the rear of the town; and besides the few straggling houses shown in the picture, and which com-

---

1. Charles C. Nahl (1818–1878) was a German-born artist—from a family of artists— who arrived in California in 1850 with his half-brother Hugo. The two tried their hand at gold mining, then settled in San Francisco to pursue their trade as lithographers, photographers, and commercial illustrators. Charles Nahl is best known as one who created vast, colorful canvases that epitomize the California Gold Rush.

prise the Pueblo of Yerba Buena, the only signs of life in either sketch is a solitary ship sailing up the bay.

I can imagine this ship to be the old *Brooklyn*[2] of New York, whose ribs now lie rotting on the beach at Aspinwall[3]—the old *Brooklyn* of Mormon fame, which, on the afternoon of July 31st, 1846—just such a bright, breezy day as my pioneer picture shows—entered these almost solitary headlands and dropped her anchor off just such a lifeless little town. And, standing on those hills in the rear at sunset, just as I did then, but not without many misgivings as to my safety from fancied wild beasts in the sand bush, and a spice of real danger from native guerrillas, believed to be hovering in the vicinity—the little, quaint town lies spread out at my feet, while to the left I see over a desolate, gray waste the bold shores of the entrance to the bay, the low walls of the Presidio buildings alone intervening to rescue the scene from barbaric wilderness.

The town of Yerba Buena, I said, lies beneath me; that is, below a point of observation which my memory fixes at or near the head of Jackson street. The dense growth of dwarfed and wind-flattened shrubbery covering these hills extended down within three hundred feet of the plaza, or about the line of Dupont street.[4] This brush was the cover of coyotes and rabbits, wildcats, and sometimes larger game, and was inhabited by innumerable quail, whose answering calls on that memorable first sunset walk I can even now hear through all the lapse of time. On my left arises Russian hill, so named from the Russian burial ground nearly at its top, and plainly marked by the black wooden crosses planted irregularly over half an acre. The road to the Presidio crosses the "divide" just below this, and is the only beaten highway leading out of town except the Mission road, through the sand, starting from the junction of California and Kearny streets.

Opposite where I stand is Telegraph hill, whose name comes later into

---

2. Sam Brannan was the "Elder" at the head of a group of 238 Mormons that arrived in Yerba Buena on the *Brooklyn* on July 31, 1846, expecting to find themselves in virgin territory—a place for them to establish their own colony and to be the predominant force—but were astonished to find themselves still under American dominance. The United States had taken control some three weeks earlier.
3. Aspinwall was the original name for Colon, the Atlantic terminus of the Panama Railroad—for William Henry Aspinwall (1807–1875), one of the founders of the Pacific Mail Steamship Co. Entrepreneurial necessity drove Aspinwall and his partners to build a railroad across the Isthmus of Panama. Construction began in 1850, and the first train ran in 1853. The railroad was forty-seven and a half miles long and cost $7.5 million.
4. Now Grant Street.

history than the period whereof I write. Not a solitary structure breaks its bald outline. Stay, here are a few houses of the dead on its eastern face, and there at its foot, in the smooth lawn stretching towards Washerwoman's bay [lagoon]. The eye drops gratefully into this verdant miniature valley between Russian and Telegraph peaks. It is the only strip of lawn in the near landscape, and the only spot making any pretensions to pastoral pleasantness. An adobe house on the shore of the lagoon just this side of the line of the white sand beach, is the only habitation in this section, or north of a line drawn from the street on which I am standing to the base of Telegraph hill. A garden and farm yard, or "corral," adjoin the adobe, and a few cattle are feeding along the shores of the lagoon. The nearest structure to me is a dilapidated windmill, the tower built of the ubiquitous adobe. Its sails have long since been strewn on the wings of the Summer winds, which are piping high and musically on this afternoon of my first visit, but not then as at this time laden with dust and grit. This windmill and a house adjoining became in the year following that of which I write the office of the second newspaper printed in Yerba Buena. Let us mark the spot as we go along. The *Californian*, begun in Monterey, was moved to Yerba Buena, and published by the tallest man in the country, from this adobe windmill.

Just this side the windmill there is a deep gully extending from the hills in the rear to a lagoon at the foot of Jackson street on the shores of the bay. This lagoon, which is fed by springs from out a strip of marshy ground just above, but chiefly nourished by the tides that steal through the narrow sandy barrier separating it from the bay, skirts the base of Telegraph hill on the north and nearly reaches Washington street on the south. The sandy beach that forms its eastern boundary marks the line of that memorable indentation which at high tide gave us boat landings within thirty yards of Montgomery street, all along the city front from Washington to Sacramento streets. I have said that these were the days when San Francisco was a "little cove." Sweeping onwards along the rocky ledge, known afterwards as Clark's point, this shore line flattens out, as we have just noted, into a sand-spit at the lagoon, touches high ground again at Washington street and extends as a broad beach to the foot of California street, where it skirts another salt marsh covered with "chaparral." Here, also, is the outlet of another wide ravine coming down from the hills in the rear. Beyond this marsh the beach stretches away, a narrow margin of white sand fringed with overhanging banks covered with dense shrubbery, and at last completes the semi-circle of the city's front at Rincon point. This was the shore line when San Francisco was surveyed, its streets laid out, and its lots and blocks marked and numbered on the city map. The actual frontage of the town of Yerba Buena, however, terminated off the salt marsh just mentioned, and the settlement was chiefly gathered on the broad plateau sloping down from the edge of the "bush" at Dupont street to the bay, and by the Jackson street and California street ravines.

And now there rises on the evening air the howl of a coyote from among the graves on Russian hill, and by a remarkable coincidence of circumstances I am at the same instant reminded that it is full time to retrace my steps down the slope towards the town. As I descend, the eye takes in the straggling, squat habitations of men in something like this order: A good sized adobe, facing the bay, a little back from the line of Dupont street and in the middle of the block, occupies the most commanding elevation of all the houses in town. It is built like most adobes in those days, one story and two rooms, only it enjoys the superior privilege of a shingle roof and a floor of boards instead of native earth. This house gave the first shelter to the *Brooklyn* colony of Mormons, and was occupied by them until the company was broken up and its members scattered, when it came into pleasant village notoriety as the "adobe store" of Robert A. Parker, a genial Boston man and enterprising merchant. Lower down and in the block between Clay and Washington streets, just above the Plaza, were two or three other frame dwellings, the best of which, a neat frame cottage with broad verandah, owned by Captain Smith of Bodega, was leased by Brannan shortly after he landed from the *Brooklyn*. This house stood just in the rear of the famous old adobe custom-house on the northwest corner of the Plaza. I can see the long, low, red-tiled roof overhanging the spacious balcony stretching from end to end of the old adobe, and the marine with his musket pacing to and fro under the shadow of the flagstaff in front—and I can hear the slatting of the halyards against the pole, as the flag streams out and vibrates in the afternoon breeze—all as plainly as though it were but yesterday. Northwest of the Plaza the nearest building was a little red one-story cottage, built by old Captain Cooper, just across the street (but a little lower down) from the adobe custom-house, the first office of the *Alta California* years later. Vacant lots intervened up to the line of Jackson street, where, just above the intersection of Kearny, a few straggling tenements—one, if I remember rightly, an adobe dwelling, arrested the eye in that direction, and a frame house or two stood facing the bay on Kearny street. Still further to the north and west, beyond the ravine and not far from the base of Telegraph hill, was a grog shop kept by an old character whom we knew as Tinker, a good-natured English castaway, who persisted that he was "growing younger every day," until one morning when his little den was opened Death was found to have stopped the backward flight of the old man's years. This groggery and one or two small houses near by furnished up the town in that quarter, and we may turn our face eastward again.

John Fuller's house and garden were the most prominent objects below Kearny street, south of Washington. The lots were neatly inclosed, and if I remember rightly, his was the only piece of tilled ground within the limits of the town proper. In the block between Washington and Clay streets, back of the line of Montgomery street, were several structures, the most noteworthy of which was a neat adobe residence on Washington street, occupied by Peter Sherreback, and a frame grist-mill (mule power) standing on the line of Clay street. Into the second story of this mill, up a rickety flight of steps on the outside, was moved, in August, the first printing office landed on these shores, and here the press was first set up and put in operation. In the same month the *Californian* was started at Monterey. There is just a question if the first news sheet issued in the English language was not printed on this press and published from this mill. But be this as it may, let it be noted among the little incidents of early times, that the two pioneers of San Francisco were each started in a grist-mill. While the type were being set in the loft for the first sheet—the extra in advance of the California *Star,* containing an account of Gen. Taylor's first battles on the Rio Grande—a mule was grinding out the meal on the ground floor below, on which a part of the towns people were fed.

The *Sacramento Daily Union,* September 16, 1871

As these sketches of memorable localities in San Francisco in the year whereof I write are nothing if not accurate, it will save trouble, perhaps, to correct misprints as we go along. "Let it be recorded," therefore, that John Fuller's house and garden was the most notable object in the square between Kearny and Montgomery streets, north of Washington street, and not south of it, as the printer made me say in my first article. I hasten to anticipate, also, another cavil which some veteran pioneer might with propriety interpose to the statement that Fuller's garden was the only piece of tilled ground within the limits of the town proper. There were other cultivated patches, as some one may rise up and say, but I stand by my "metes and bounds." The town proper of those nursing days was cuddled in the lap of that broad slope of hard native earth extending down from Dupont street to the beach thirty yards below Montgomery street, and bounded north and south by the two ravines that came down from the hills about on the lines of Jackson and California streets. Between these gullies, therefore, behold the town proper of Yerba Buena. The half-breed babe—the half Mexican and half "foreign" prodigy, whose infant lineaments are scarcely recognizable in the stately San Francisco. Outside of these limits it all was "suburban"—pastoral—wild.

And as yet we have not reached the heart of this town. Like all proper anatomies it had that indispensable organ, with all its functional appurtenances. Its lungs we shall call the plaza, then much more frequently called Portsmouth Square, in honor of the gallant sloop of war whose marines garrisoned the town. Its right, upper and lower chambers we shall "locate," in the two billiard rooms—the City Hotel on the southeast corner of the square west of Kearny street, and the Portsmouth House, fifty paces down Clay street on the same (south) side of the way. The left or distributing reservoirs of this organ of collective life shall be Montgomery street, west side, from Sacramento street north to Washington.

Leidesdorff's Hotel, afterwards known as the City Hotel, with its billiard room, was the pivotal center of social life in those times. It was the largest house in town, to begin with. It was the first house in town, both in the order of respectability and by virtue of its location, at the entrance of the place, on the only highway leading in from the interior—the Monterey, or more familiarly styled, the Mission road. It was also at the head of navigation for midshipmen ashore "on a lark," and for an occasional man-o'-war's man when he chanced to miss his bearings on the north side of town, where the sailor "pulperias" stood, and strike the bar of the City Hotel. Let the Leidesdorff hostelry therefore stand forth!

A "long, low" (long may these piratical adjectives wave!), wide-balconied, shingle-roof adobe. fronting on Kearny street, with an "L" extending forty or fifty feet westward along Clay. In the south end was the large billiard room and its two tables and its eight balls that were never still day or night, except in the "wee, sma'" hours of midnight. Adjoining this was the bar room, and on the opposite side again, the little room off for monte, without which I suppose a Mexican hostelry would be simply inhospitable. In the middle of the long building was the dining hall, the largest room in town, and pre-eminent for its fitness for fandangoes and late suppers. Parlors, of course, the Leidesdorff Hotel had none, and the remainder of the space on the ground floor was divided up into sleeping rooms and offices. This wonderful center of social life on the Bay of San Francisco was a story and a half in height, the attic being used for lodging rooms. It was kept at the time of which I am writing by a dapper Englishman, whom we called "Brown"—John H. Brown. Leidesdorff, the builder and owner of the house, and I may say in passing, the life and soul of the town, lived in a cottage at the foot of California street. The offices in the City Hotel fronting on Washington street were occupied first as headquarters of the naval commander of the district, and afterward by lawyers, surveyors, and others. There were then no other houses on the south side of the square; and beyond the City Hotel the only house on Kearny street before coming to the California street ravine was the Mexican ranch of our worthy and esteemed townsman, John J. Vioget, a gentleman, scholar, and surveyor. Vioget was the first to survey and lay off the town of San Francisco, and his work was afterward incorporated into the more general survey made by Jasper O'Farrell.

Across the way from the Leidesdorff or City Hotel stood an adobe building with a blind wall abutting the street. It was an old ranch, which had probably been built before the town was laid out, and it was the only structure on the south side of Washington street east of Kearny, except the Portsmouth House, a few yards below. This well remembered public resort stood with its gable end to the street, and its largest and best room was devoted to billiards and bar. I cannot remember that it had any sleeping rooms, though there must have been lodging places in an extension running parallel with Washington street, for here was the dining hall. It was like a young robin, all mouth and eyes; its large billiard room and bright bottles swallowing up one's first look and thought. This hotel was kept in the Fall and Winter of 1846 by a gentleman whose name shall be no more illustrious in mere nomenclature than that of the proprietor of the rival establishment—Brown. Mine host of the Portsmouth bore the name of Jones! Brown & Jones—Jones & Brown!

And here in the hostelries of Brown and Jones, gathered after nightfall in the two billiard rooms, sending the balls right and left, tossing off their *bueno salutos* in foreign wines or native aguadiente, smoking their long-nines, cheroots, and cigarettos, listlessly cutting their names on chair-backs and window-sills, or dozing in corner seats, survey the townspeople of this lively, gossipy, Yankee, British, German, Russian, and Mexican town. While the ships of war lay in port, there was usually a midshipman or other brass-buttoned valiant at the end of every cue, and citizens ranged like wall-flowers idly watching the game and discussing village topics; or at other times there would be an arrival of strangers from Monterey or further down the coast; or, rarer and more welcome still, new comers from the States by way of the plains, or in some Boston or New York ship, to give interest and zest to the evening's chat. Here were the exchanges, after the work of the day was done, for all the news both of the little corner of the earth in which we were shut up and the great, wide world, often a six months' journey distant beyond mountains and seas.

We come at last to Montgomery street—then the Wall and Water street, the Broadway and boulevard of the future San Francisco. Let us count its commercial houses and shops, beginning on the south of the line, and know, O reader, that in our enumeration we shall not cross the street. Our census begins and ends on the west side, for the simple reason that its eastern row of stores and warehouses were somehow away off in the golden pathway of the rising sun, which every morning shot his beams from the level of the hills over the bay, full on the unobstructed front of the sleeping town, flooding Montgomery street from its western line of stores to the broad sand beach beneath with an unbroken blaze. The most shining mark of this city front was the store of Howard & Mellus, a neat white frame building, formerly occupied by the Russian Consul, near what is now the intersection of Sacramento with Montgomery. It was, like each of the other commercial houses of the town, both store and dwelling. The firm was the most popular and enterprising in the place, and stood at the head of the little business which the town was doing. Howard & Mellus were both Boston men, who had drifted to the coast in hide-droghers years before. Their store was small, and their stock of goods light; selected, of course, for the native trash chiefly, and comprising every staple necessary of life in a wild region.

The ground adjoining the building occupied by them comprised several 150-vara lots, and was neatly inclosed from the verandah of the store to the corner of Clay, and thence up Washington street to the Portsmouth House. Not a solitary structure broke the line of this inclosure; but in the center of the fenced area, which was covered with grass, I remember, there was the grave of the Russian Consul, and it was told how he had ended his career a short time before by suicide.

At the corner of Clay street, north side, we resume our count, "pegging" two for the store of W. H. Davis, which we shall see presently was its rightful number. Davis was a bustling, but not over popular body, from the Sandwich Islands. He had acquired the sobriquet of "Kanaka Davis;" but if there was Hawaiian blood in his veins it had not impaired his Yankee vigor and sharpness. His store was one of a little cluster of adobe buildings north of Clay street. It stood back from the street, was neatly inclosed and white-washed, and although a low and inconvenient structure, like most adobes, presented a picturesque appearance. A twin building next door, separated by a low board fence, was the store of the new firm of Ward & Smith. Ward was a passenger from New York in the ship *Brooklyn,* and Smith, the most jovial, popular man in town, did not disdain the nickname, by which his best friends knew him, of "Jim Crow Smith." He came by it cleverly, for he was inimitable as a delineator of negro character, and possessed the rare faculty of doing it in a gentlemanly way. Smith was the life of the little private gatherings of gentlemen in the quiet town. And this store of Ward & Smith, counting number three in our list, ends the chapter of Montgomery street merchants in 1846.

There was a shop and residence, if I remember rightly, adjoining Ward & Smith's on the north, just before you come to Clay. But my census is complete of the commercial men doing business on our water front between Sacramento and Washington. The Spring of 1847 added another name to the list and extended the line of stores to the north corner of Montgomery and Washington streets. At this time a frame building was erected and filled with goods, and the new firm of Roland, Gelston & Co., afterwards C. L. Ross & Co., came into existence. Their goods were brought from New York in the bark *Whiton,* and first offered for sale in a rude, temporary building erected on the beach. The first store which crossed Montgomery street and occupied the east side of the street was the establishment of Sherman & Ruckel, which took its place among the houses of our frail commercial colony in the early part of 1847.

A Map of the Town of San Francisco, 1847.

Known variously as the Alcalde map, Bartlett's map, and Buckalew's map. It was made in December 1846 or January 1847, apparently copied from an 1843 "Plan of Yerba Buena," which itself was based on Vioget's Yerba Buena map of 1839. This served as the official map for only a brief time, since Alcalde Bartlett in November 1846 had requested Jasper O'Farrell to resurvey the town. Bartlett was absent on business at the time this map was prepared. When he returned, in January, he gave the map its title, named the streets, and certified it as the official town map. This is a redone, cleaned-up version of the original, which is creased, stained, and difficult to decipher. The original is in the California State Library in Sacramento.

San Francisco, Upper California, in 1847.
Drawn on stone by Victor Prevost.

The article beginning on the opposite page, with its accompanying map, was first printed in 1937 as a sixteen-page pamphlet, in a somewhat abbreviated form, in a limited edition of one hundred copies, for private distribution. It was reprinted in 1957. The complete version appeared in the December 1938 issue of the *California Historical Society Quarterly,* and I am reprinting it with the permission of the California Historical Society.

Because some sixty years have passed since the article was published, some of the descriptions and citations are no longer valid. I have inserted new information in brackets to indicate the changes of the intervening six decades. I have also omitted several passages that are not relevant to the main topic of the article.

The reason that the map of old Yerba Buena bears the date of January 30, 1847 is because that was considered, at the time, to be the official date that the village of Yerba Buena was renamed San Francisco—since the notice of the name change appeared on that date, in English and Spanish, in *The California Star,* the only newspaper then published in Yerba Buena. But the identical notice also was printed in that paper on January 23. Neither of these notices was dated.

In the *San Francisco Call* of September 8, 1901 there was an article on the origin of Yerba Buena/San Francisco, its early settlement, the first surveys, and the origin of street names. In the course of the article the author casually stated that "Alcalde Bartlett had by proclamation, dated January 19, 1847, changed the name of the village of Yerba Buena to that of San Francisco." One can only assume that the original proclamation of Bartlett, properly dated, had been seen by the author or was generally known to exist and to have that date upon it—and that it was destroyed, along with other municipal records, in the earthquake and fire of 1906.

An Hour's Walk through Yerba Buena

Which Later Became San Francisco[1]

To most Californians, even to many who live in San Francisco, there is an indefiniteness about the very village of Yerba Buena from which the present-day city of San Francisco has grown. Few will be found who can describe the settlement's location, let alone its boundaries. Fewer still know how it came into being. To satisfy the widespread curiosity regarding San Francisco's humble beginnings, let us endeavor to erase the changes that one hundred and three years have wrought. Let us obliterate all that is familiar to us and to try in our imaginations, to picture that portion of San Francisco bounded by Pine Street on the south, Broadway on the north, Stockton Street on the west, and Leidesdorff Street on the east—without streets, buildings, or people. The uneven terrain within our view would be covered with sagebrush, lupine, and wild mint, the plant the Mexicans knew by the name of *Yerba Buena,* which on account of its profuseness gave to the spot the designation of *Paraje de Yerba Buena,* or the place of wild mint.

What we have created in fancy was the actuality that confronted Captain William Antonio Richardson on the afternoon of June 25, 1835, when with his wife, Maria Antonia Martinez, and their three children, he unloaded his pack animals on the slope of the hills rising from the cove that nestled between the base of Loma Alta—the height we call Telegraph Hill today—and Rincon Point.

Armed with a map of his projected settlement and the approval of Governor Figueroa, Richardson's first concern was to shelter his family, and this he did by erecting a tent fashioned from an old sail. The town-

---

1. The superior numbers in the text refer to the places marked on the map.

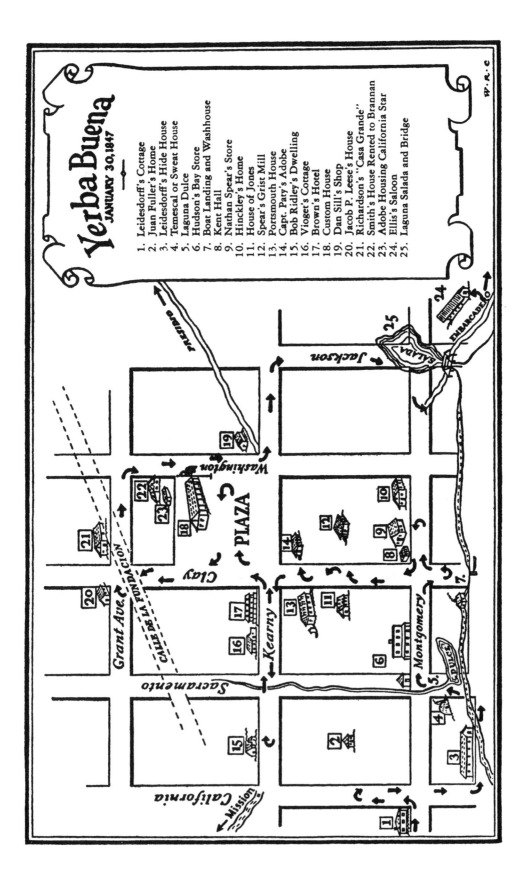

Yerba Buena
JANUARY 30, 1847

1. Leidesdorff's Cottage
2. Juan Fuller's Home
3. Leidesdorff's Hide House
4. Temescal or Sweat House
5. Laguna Dulce
6. Hudson's Bay Store
7. Boat Landing and Washhouse
8. Kent Hall
9. Nathan Spear's Store
10. Hinckley's Home
11. House of Jones
12. Spear's Grist Mill
13. Portsmouth House
14. Capt. Pary's Adobe
15. Bob Ridley's Dwelling
16. Vioget's Cottage
17. Brown's Hotel
18. Custom House
19. Dan Sill's Shop
20. Jacob P. Leese's House
21. Richardson's "Casa Grande"
22. Smith's House Rented to Brannan
23. Adobe Housing California Star
24. Ellis's Saloon
25. Laguna Salada and Bridge

W. R. C

founder knew the climate, for, following his arrival in San Francisco Bay as mate of the British whaler *Orion* in 1822, and his marriage to a daughter of Lieutenant Ignacio Martinez in 1825, he had lived a number of years at the Presidio. To protect his household from the storms of winter, the tent was insufficient, and in October he built a rough board shack to take the place of his first habitation. It was this crude building that Richard Henry Dana, Jr. saw and described in *Two Years Before the Mast*, the epic of California's pastoral era.

Richardson laid out a one-street town, and called that thoroughfare "Calle de la Fundacion,"—Foundation Street, upon which and to which, presumably, all future streets would be oriented. It was an angling road, joining the trail to the Mission near today's intersection of Kearny and California streets, and the trail to the Presidio near the junction of Pacific and Stockton streets. For a whole year Richardson's family lived in lonesome seclusion. Then in July 1836 the town's second settler—Jacob Primer Leese—made his appearance, put up a board shack on the lot adjoining Richardson's on the south, and celebrated the occasion by inviting the whole countryside to a glorious Fourth of July party, at which the guests ate, danced, and drank for three days, while both the Mexican national emblem and the Stars and Stripes floated overhead.

We have set the scene. Let it serve as a background while we direct our steps through the busy streets of the San Francisco of today, stopping from time to time to call on, in fancy, the more prominent personages who created the town from which our city grew.

Our walk begins at the southwest corner of Montgomery and California streets where the Clunie Building [Bank of America] now stands.[1] Here in the early 1840s a cockney by the name of Robert Ridley built a cottage. Ridley could have qualified for membership in any liars' club: he was a teller of tall tales, besides being Yerba Buena's champion two-fisted drinker. One morning, meeting William Heath Davis, he casually asked the merchant known far and wide as "Kanaka" Davis (the nickname was due to his partial Polynesian ancestry) how many "London Docks" he imagined the speaker had downed before breakfast that day. The exact nature of this alcoholic concoction is today a mystery. Davis hazarded, "Five or six." Such a small quantity was an insult; it challenged Ridley's capacity. "Why, I've gotten away with twenty-three, and I think I'll take another before I eat, just to whet my appetite." Ridley had married Presentacion Miranda, the daughter of the famous Juana Briones Miranda, who kept cows and lived on her small ranch at Powell and Filbert streets at North Beach. William H. Thomes, who wrote of his experiences under the title of *On Land and Sea*, tells of Juana and her milk and the difficulty of finding a receptacle in which to carry some back to the ship. Juana solved the problem, but shocked the lad serving before the mast. [Thomes was so shocked that he couldn't bring himself to name the receptacle. Apparently it was a chamber pot.] . . . Ridley worked as a clerk for the Hudson's Bay Company, and in 1846 sold his cottage, which had the only flower garden in the town, to William Alexander Leidesdorff, a part-Negro Dane from the town of Saint Croix in the West Indies, who had come to California in 1841 as master of the schooner *Julia Ann*.

Leidesdorff moved in, and his pretty half-caste Alaskan-Russian house-keeper helped him entertain and keep up the dignity of being United States vice-consul. As a merchant, Leidesdorff succeeded, and acquired real estate, including the Natomas Grant on the American River. At the time of his death, in May 1848, he was land poor and practically bankrupt, which made it possible for Captain Joseph L. Folsom to purchase the entire holdings for less than one hundred thousand dollars, and consequently become the city's wealthiest citizen.

Across California Street, on the site now occupied by the San Francisco Bank [550 California Street, built in 1959],[2] lived Jack Fuller with his Mexican wife and children. He, like Richardson and Ridley, was an Englishman. Yerba Buena's outstanding man of all trades, he was not only laundryman, cook, and butcher, but for a time served the town as its *sindico* or treasurer. Juan was the first man to spend the community's money for street improvement, a matter of ten dollars for clipping off the overhanging boughs of trees that endangered travelers on the trail to the Mission. But Fuller's fame rests upon a much more secure foundation: he it was who was responsible for changing the name Yerba Buena Island to Goat Island. In 1842, Captain Gorham H. Nye sailed the *Fama* into San Francisco Bay. Fuller discovered that Nye had goats, both billies and nannies, on board. To Nathan Spear, merchant and the best-liked man in the town, he proposed a purchase of the livestock. Spear was cajoled into the business by Fuller's description of roasted kid to relieve the monotonous beef diet to which the residents of Yerba Buena were condemned. Lack of fences decided the buyers to place the animals on the island, where they multiplied exceedingly.

The Trust Department of the American Trust Company [Wells Fargo Bank], on the northwest corner of California and Leidesdorff streets, marks the spot where Leidesdorff had his hide warehouse.[3] Small draught schooners could come alongside, and there the hides gathered from the rancheros about the Bay were stored until sold to Boston ships for transportation to the Atlantic seaboard. Where Sacramento Street crosses Montgomery, the Indian crew of Richardson's schooner maintained a *te-*

mescal, or sweat house.[4] Here was a sweetwater lagoon fed by a rivulet that coursed down today's Sacramento Street, from scrub-oak-filled ravines in the hills on the west.[5] Into this fresh-water lake at the beach the Indians would plunge after their torrid stays in the *temescal.*

Mention has been made of the coming to Yerba Buena of Jacob Primer Leese. He was an American, and in his merchandising venture he had two partners, William Sturgis Hinckley and Nathan Spear, both of whom were American born. A quarrel with his absent partners over profits—Spear was at Monterey and Hinckley was at sea as captain of the *Corsair*—led to a dissolution of the partnership and the coming of Spear and Hinckley to Yerba Buena. From Governor Alvarado, Leese obtained the easterly two-thirds of the block now bounded by Montgomery, Clay, Kearny, and Sacramento streets, and there built a combined house and place of business.[6] In 1837 he had married Rosalia Vallejo, the General's sister, and in 1841 he sold out to the Hudson's Bay Company and removed to Sonoma, where his brother-in-law ruled with unquestioned authority over countless acres of land and herds of cattle without number. The main structure of Leese's second Yerba Buena building venture stood fronting what was to become in later years Montgomery Street. A hide warehouse occupied more than half of what is now Sacramento Street. Here the great Hudson's Bay trading establishment went about its avowed purpose of seizing the entire California business of barter. William Glen Rae was the factor in charge. His wife, Eloise, the half-breed daughter of the great Dr. John McLoughlin, who presided over the destinies of the company at Fort Vancouver on the Columbia River, kept house and entertained the important personages who called upon her hard-drinking husband. An error of judgment led Rae in 1845 to back the wrong horse in the struggle of Governor Micheltorena against Castro and Alvarado. This, and drink, were responsible for Rae's suicide when Micheltorena lost. Rae was buried in the orchard in the back of the house. Years later, when a sewer was placed in Commercial Street, which now runs through the block, Rae's coffin was unearthed. With Rae's death the Hudson's Bay Company withdrew from Yerba Buena, selling the property to two Boston men who had grown to manhood in the hide and tallow business in California—Henry Mellus and William Davis Merry Howard, whose firm name was Mellus and Howard, and who afterward became the most important merchants in the town.

The corner of Leidesdorff and Clay streets recalls many happenings of the past. Here the low cliff that went by the Spanish name of *cantil* reached its maximum height of ten feet. North and south from this point it gradually lessened. Between it and the waters of the Bay was a strip of sandy beach, and here Juan Fuller erected his washhouse,[7] close to an *ojo de agua,* or spring, which gushed forth from the *cantil* with a plentiful supply of water. Here too was a tiny wharf, where ships' boats could land at high tide, and on the solid ground above, Juan Fuller had put up a gallows-frame where as butcher he slaughtered cattle for the town's use. And here, on the memorable July 9, 1846, Captain John B. Montgomery landed his seventy sailors and marines, who marched to the Plaza, raised the Stars and Stripes, and took possession in the name of the United States of America.

When the Leese, Spear, and Hinckley firm dissolved, Nathan Spear wished to locate as near his former partner, Jacob, as possible. Land could be granted only to Mexican citizens. Spear would not change his allegiance. Here was a barrier to his desires, but he got around it by having a friend receive the grant and then transfer the land to him. His holding is today the northwest corner of Clay and Montgomery streets. There he landed a ship's house that he had bought from the captain of the bark *Kent*, and which was subsequently known as "Kent Hall."[8] Immediately adjoining it on the north he built a house.[9] When Spear retired from active business he rented his place to his nephew, William Heath Davis, who has already been mentioned. Kent Hall was the gathering spot in Yerba Buena for all choice spirits, and there many a ship's captain was entertained. At these feasts Juan Fuller presided in his capacity as cook, for it was conceded that Juan was the "cordon bleu" of California.

The Hinckley house, which stood where the southwest corner of Montgomery and Merchant streets[10] is today, was Yerba Buena's first City Hall under the American régime. Captain Montgomery, of the U.S. Sloop-of-war *Portsmouth*, appointed Washington A. Bartlett, one of his lieutenants, as chief magistrate or alcalde. Hinckley had died, and from Susana, his widow, a daughter of old Ignacio Martinez, Bartlett rented the old home and moved in to govern the town.

Clay Street between Montgomery and Kearny is replete with memories of the past and with tales of Yerba Buena's early inhabitants. Behind Kent Hall and his store, Nathan Spear built a mule-power grist mill.[12] It was halfway up the block and it was run by an old mountaineer and blacksmith whose place of business, when not working for Spear, was on the corner of Kearny and Washington streets.[19] This man was Daniel Sill, who had a reputation for being a marvelous shot. To young William Heath Davis, when time hung heavy on their hands, old Dan would say, "Willie, get the old white horse, the deer horse, and we'll go out and shoot a buck." Davis relates that their hunting ground was about where the Bay Bridge terminal now is, and that they never failed to find their game browsing on the oak-covered hillsides of what later was known as Rincon Hill. In this grist mill, wheat from the Ranchos about the Bay was ground, and here, after the coming of the ship *Brooklyn* with Sam Brannan and his two hundred-odd Mormons on July 31, 1846, Edward Cleveland Kemble, the town's first printer, a non-Mormon but one of the company, set up the press Brannan had brought with him. In the old mill the first printing in the town was done: notices for the Alcalde and some very ornate blue satin badges for the welcoming committee appointed to greet Commodore Stockton upon his arrival on October 5, 1846.

Across the way lived Elbert P. Jones,[11] who passed as a doctor, an editor, and a hotel keeper, with real estate as a sideline, and it was from him that Jones Street takes its name. Yerba Buena's streets went without names until early in 1847, when Jasper O'Farrell mapped them. Until then there was no need for designations, for the population of the town was small. Before Sam Brannan's Mormons crowded into the settlement, there were but seventy-three Mexican and Indian inhabitants and forty-eight persons of Anglo-American and non-Spanish descent. Jones's activities are so intermingled with others more important than he that his story will be revealed when mention is made of John Henry Brown and Sam Brannan.

Now we come to the heart of the community, the Portsmouth House,[13] where every notable was certain to be found if he were in Yerba Buena. The story behind this first of California hotels must be related in detail so that a proper appreciation may be had of the importance of what went on within its portals. The first picture we have of Yerba Buena, the town of 1837 with its two houses, was from the hands of a Swiss sea captain, the master of the Ecuadorian bark *Delmira,* one Jean Jacques Vioget, a man of parts if ever there was one. He was many things besides being a mariner. He played the violin, he painted, he was an engineer and surveyor, and the town voted him a jolly good fellow when he decided to leave the sea and keep a saloon. When the house of public entertainment that he built on the south side of Clay Street, about seventy feet east of Kearny, was opened for business, it possessed the only billiard table in town. Bob Ridley, out of a job after Rae's death, induced Vioget to rent the place to him, and it was there that John Henry Brown began his career of catering to the public as assistant barkeeper. . . .

Brown was indebted to the warrant officers of the U. S. S. *Portsmouth* for the naming of the hotel. They called upon him when he announced that he was about to give the town its first hostelry, and agreed to make him an up-to-the-minute signboard if he would call his establishment after their ship. Business was so good from the day the house opened that John Henry saw possibilities in expansion. Vice-Consul Leidesdorff had just built a two-story structure on what is today the southwest corner of

Kearny and Clay streets.[17] Brown rented it, converted it into "Brown's Hotel," and sold the Portsmouth House to Elbert P. Jones, who in order to be certain that his culinary department would be run properly, forthwith married Sarah Kittleman, the cook. Henceforth Yerba Buena had two hotels.

Across the way from the Porstmouth House, Captain John Paty built himself an adobe[14] for his use when he was not in command of the *Don Quixote*. During his lifetime, Paty claimed that he had made more trips between the Hawaiian Islands and California than any man alive. He was a jolly soul whom everybody liked. As we end our tramp through the Yerba Buena that was, we shall have occasion to speak again of "the senior commodore of the Royal Hawaiian Navy."

After Brown blossomed out as the proprietor of the hotel bearing his name, so many things happened that it is difficult to select one from among the many to show how life was lived in the community during its very interesting early days. South of the hotel on the west side of Kearny Street, Vioget had built himself a small house;[16] and a block farther to the southward, Bob Ridley lived after he had sold his cottage to Leidesdorff.[15] Beyond Ridley's place all was solitude through which the trail to the Mission led; but in the Plaza, bounded as it is today by Clay, Kearny, and Washington streets, with Brenham Place to the west, stood the Mexican Custom House,[18] a one-story adobe, roofed with tile and having a covered porch facing east. . . .

While Yerba Buena was still Yerba Buena and before it had become San Francisco, the Plaza was a bare clay area, devoid of trees and grass, a mud hole in winter and the source of the dust that the summer winds blew about. Nor were the streets much better. After the raising of the American flag, the Plaza took on a new name: Portsmouth Square. This is but an example of the consistent endeavor of the officers of the armed forces of the United States to obliterate all Spanish designations. Fortunately the old names have persisted, so that we still have San Jose instead of St. Joseph, San Juan instead of St. John, and Los Angeles in place of Angels, though in their reports and letters the officials mentioned consistently used the translated designations.

Having toiled up Clay Street from the site of "Brown's Hotel," we may take our stand on what today is the southeast corner of that thoroughfare and Grant Avenue. To all San Franciscans this is sacred ground, for here within a hundred feet of us is the cradle of a great city. Richardson's *Calle de la Fundacion* crossed the intersection before us, and the site of his tent, his rough board shack and his great adobe built in 1837, called the "Casa

Grande,"[21] is now occupied by the stores of Chinese merchants whose quarters line the western side of Grant Avenue north of Clay Street.

The southwest corner, across from us, is where Jacob Primer Leese built Yerba Buena's second house[20] in 1836, though the plaque fastened to the present building would have you believe that Leese was the first to build a habitation in the new town. [The plaque no longer exists.] The misinformation does not stop there, for it tells that the first white child born in the city of San Francisco saw the light of day at this spot. While it is true that Rosalia Leese was the first white child born in Yerba Buena, yet fifty-nine years before her advent, children of white Spanish parents were born and baptized at the Mission of San Francisco de Asis, which today lies within the city limits. The only statement on the plaque that cannot be challenged is that the American flag was displayed here for the first time on that glorious Fourth of July, 1836.

And now we will walk north one block to Washington Street and down it to the right until we reach the China Exchange, the delightful oriental building housing the telephone company's plant that serves Chinatown.[22] [Now the Bank of Canton of California.] Here stood the pretentious white house of Captain Stephen Smith, who brought California her first pianos.

Sam Brannan, when he left New York with his Mormons in the ship *Brooklyn* on the 4th of February 1846, had, prior to sailing, prepared everything necessary for the publication of a newspaper in the far-off land of California. Even the name of the journal had been chosen, and a stereotype had been made of the masthead to adorn the paper's front page.

The California Star did not shine in the promised land, however, until five months after the party landed, and in the meantime Printer Kemble went off to the war in the southern region about Los Angeles, as a member of Frémont's California Battalion. Brannan needed quarters for himself and his activities as a Mormon elder. He rented Stephen Smith's house, and after moving in he erected a small abobe building in the back yard in which to house his printing plant.[23] The press was removed from Spear's grist mill, and all was made ready for a start as New Year's Day 1847 drew near. . . . While the press was still housed in the grist mill, Kemble had run off a prospectus in advance of publication. . . . The date printed on this notice was October 24, 1846, but Yerba Buena had to wait for January 9, 1847 before seeing its first hometown paper. . . .

Down Washington Street our Yerba Buena tour now takes us. As we turn north into Kearny Street we pass the corner where Dan Sill worked at his forge[19] and where a trail led over the hills through the *puerto suelo*, today's Pacific Avenue between Taylor and Leavenworth streets, to the Presidio. At Jackson Street we turn again, this time to our right, and follow down the south side of that thoroughfare. Before us let us imagine the Laguna Salada,[25] the salt-water lagoon, joined by a tidal inlet with Yerba Buena Cove. In fancy let us cross it by the bridge, the first of San Francisco's Bay bridges, which William Sturgis Hinckley built in 1844 while he was alcalde of the town. The purpose of this improvement was to permit Yerba Buenans to walk dryshod to the embarcadero at Clark's Point—Broadway and Battery streets of today—where boats could land at all stages of the tide.

Before us, on the land just beginning to rise to form Loma Alta—our Telegraph Hill—was the saloon and boarding house run by Alfred J. Ellis,[24] frequented by both master mariners and sailors, and the locale of an incident of early days that John Henry Brown related with great gusto. Ellis had a well, twenty-four feet deep, from which he drew his water supply. Brown was a boarder, for he had just closed Brown's Hotel due to a misunderstanding with Leidesdorff, who demanded three thousand dollars a year rent instead of two thousand, which Brown said had been verbally agreed upon. The night was wet and stormy. Among the ships in the cove was a Russian barque here to load wheat for Alaska. Ellis banged on Brown's door in the early morning hours, shouting that there was a man in the well. Brown thinking it a joke or a hoax, paid no attention, but finally dressed and descended to the bar, where he found a drunken sailor, dripping from his immersion and being plied with whiskey. This sorry individual kept muttering, "The other fellow grunted something awful as we fell in," but no one paid any attention to him. A reward was offered for a Russian sailor said to have deserted from his ship. Two, three, four days elapsed, and then the remains of the deserter were found floating in the well. Captain John Paty took to his bed. He had not only qualified his whiskey with Ellis's well water but had taken it as a chaser.

Shortly after *The California Star* began publication, Doc Semple and Thomas O. Larkin, the American Consul for California, were greatly disturbed. They had bargained with General Vallejo to subdivide a part of his holdings on the Strait of Carquinez and were about to give their new town the name of Francisca in honor of the general's wife. Francisca on San Francisco Bay! That was a name to conjure with, one that would overshadow little and unknown Yerba Buena, for all the world knew the name of the greatest harbor on America's west coast. To Washington A. Bartlett, Alcalde and Yerba Buena's chief magistrate, came news of the subdividers' plans. Their nefarious scheme would have to be forestalled. Alcalde Bartlett went into executive session, then with a freshly cut quill he wrote the epochal decision that forced Larkin and Semple to give Senora Vallejo's second name—Benicia—to their projected metropolis.

From *The California Star*, January 23, 1847

AN ORDINANCE.

Whereas the local name of Yerba Buena as applied to the settlement or town of *San Francisco*—is unknown beyond the immediate district; and has been applied from the local name of the Cove on which the town is built.—Therefore, to prevent confusion and mistakes in public documents, and that the town may have the advantage of the name given on the published maps.

It is hereby ordered that the name of *San Francisco*, shall hereafter be used in all official communications, and public documents, or records appertaining to the town.

WASH'N A. BARTLETT.
Chief Magistrate.

Published by order.

J. G. T. Dunleavy, *Municipal Clerk.*

ORDENANZA PUBLICA.

Considerando que el nombre "Yerba Buena" como aplicado al pueblo de *San Francisco* es desconocido afuera del distrito inmediato; y estaba aplicado del nombre de la playa en que el pueblo esta situado.

Por esto, a prevenir equivocos en los documentos publicos, y que el publico gozare la ventaja del nombre publicado ya en los planos y mapas; Juzgo necessario a decretar, que en adelante el nombre de *San Francisco*, sera escrito en todos communicaciones, documentos, y registros publicos; que pertenecen al pueblo de *San Francisco*.

WASH'N A. BARTLETT.
Alcalde lo Prop'o.

Publicado por orden.

J. G. T. Dunleavy, *Sect'o Municipal.*

Volume 1, No. 1 of *The California Star* was published in Yerba Buena (soon to be San Francisco) on January 9, 1847. It was the embryonic community's first newspaper.

Jasper O'Farrell (1817–1875), an Irish-born civil engineer, came to Yerba Buena in 1843. In his professional capacity he laid out a number of Mexican ranchos, and surveyed the town of Benicia— San Francisco's main competitor at the time. In November 1846, Alcalde Washington Bartlett asked O'Farrell to do a new survey of Yerba Buena/San Francisco. The existing maps of the town, which were in use for issuing lots, did not agree with the actual conditions on the ground. The streets still followed Vioget's 1839 survey: they didn't intersect at right angles, and thus no two streets or lots were parallel.

O'Farrell realigned the streets as if they were on a pivot based at the corner of Washington and Kearny streets, shifting the streets two and a half degrees in a northeast-southwest direction—a method known as "O'Farrell's swing." His major contribution to the appearance of the future metropolis was to lay out Market Street parallel to the road to the mission, and to orient the streets south of Market to this broad new boulevard. He also mapped the beach and water lots; his map of the survey, as will be seen, showed several hundred lots that were actually under water at high tide. They would eventually be filled in, and become some of San Francisco's most valuable property. O'Farrell also named the streets—amazingly, something that had not been done pre- viously—and in due time a street was named for him. His map is reproduced at the end of this chapter, on page 165.

The Progress of Yerba Buena/San Francisco

From *The California Star*, January 16, 1847

The importance of some immediate action on the part of the citizens of Yerba Buena, in reference to the establishment of a school in the place, must be apparent to every one who has passed through our principle streets, in good weather. We counted the other day, about forty children from the age of five to thirteen, in the different streets at play; who ought, instead of wasting their time in idleness, to be at school. Childhood and youth are the seasons for mental culture; the impressions then made are lasting: and the mind then being free from the cares incident to after life, is better prepared to receive knowledge and general moral improvement than at any other age. Therefore, this period of life should not be suffered to be passed in frivolous amusements or unprofitable employment. We hold it to be an inexcusable dereliction of duty on the part of parents, and those having influence and means, to suffer the children in the community in which they live to grow up in ignorance.

We mention this subject now in order to draw public attention to it; and in another number of our paper, we will suggest a plan for the immediate establishment of a school in this place, which we think cannot fail to meet the approbation of the citizens generally. We have no children, but we feel a deep interest in the proper education and moral training of the children in the country, and for the purpose of putting a school in operation, we will give one half of a lot of fifty varas square in a suitable part of the Town, and fifty dollars in money.

AN ORDINANCE (January 23)

Whereas the practice of firing guns and pistols in the town of San

Francisco and vicinity, already prohibited in the general orders of the late Com'dt. of the District, is not observed—and in consequence persons have been injured, and others endangered, while pursuing their necessary occupations.

It is therefore ordered that from and after the publication of this ordinance, any person, or persons, who shall discharge any fire arms within one mile of the Public square, shall be fined on conviction thereof, the sum of twenty dollars for each and every offence—one half of which shall be paid to the person proving the same.

As the police of the town is under the supervision of the Com'dt. of the Garrison, any person wishing to discharge their arms, will apply to him for permission to do so.

WASH'N A. BARTLETT.
Chief Magistrate.

Yerba Buena and San Francisco Bay (January 30)

Yerba Buena, the name of our town which means GOOD HERB, is situated on the south west side of the principle arm of San Francisco bay, about five miles from the ocean, on a narrow neck of land varying from four to ten miles in width. The narrowest place being sixteen miles south west of the town. It is in latitude 37° 45' north. This narrow slip of land is about sixty miles in length, extending from the point formed by the bay and the ocean, to the valley of San Jose.

The site of the town is handsome and commanding—being an inclined plain of about a mile in extent from the water's edge to the hills in the rear. Two points of land—one on each side—extending into the bay form a crescent or small bay in the shape of a crescent in front, which bears the name of the town. These points afford a fine view of the surrounding country—the snow capped mountains in the distance—the green valleys beneath them, the beautiful, smooth and unruffled bay in front and on either side, at once burst upon the eye. There is in front of the town a small Island, rising high above the surface of the bay, about two miles long and one wide, which is covered the greater part of the year with the most exuberant herbage of untrodden freshness. This little Island is about three miles from the shore. Between it and the town is the principal anchorage. Here the vessels of all nations rest in safety and peace, and their flags are displayed by the aromatic breeze. Two hundred yards from the shore there is twenty-four feet water, and a short distance beyond that, as many fathoms. The beach immediately in front of the now business part of the town is shelving; but it will no doubt in a short time be filled up and become the most valuable part of the place.

The climate here is, in the winter, which is the rainy season, damp and chilly. During the balance of the year it is dry, but chilly, in consequence of the continual strong winds from the north and north west. There is but little variation in the atmosphere throughout the year, the thermometer ranging from fifty five to seventy degrees Fahrenheit.

Yerba Buena is one of the most healthy places on the whole coast of the Pacific. Sickness of any kind is rarely known among us. The salubrity of the climate—beauty of the site of the town—its contiguity to the mouth of the bay—the finest harbor on the whole coast in front—the rich and beautiful country around it, all conspire to render it one of the best commercial points in the world.

The town is new, having been laid off in 1839 by Capt. John Vioget;— and not withstanding all the troubles in the country, has gradually increased in size and importance. It now contains a population of about five hundred permanent citizens. Two years ago there were but about two hundred.

Three miles south is the mission Dolores on Mission creek, surrounded by a small valley of rich and beautiful land. The water from this creek can easily be brought by means of aqueducts to any point to supply vessels. For the supply of the citizens the best of well water is obtained in every part of the town, by boring the distance of forty feet.

In going south from Yerba Buena, the traveller passes over this narrow neck of land; a most delightful region interspersed with hills, valleys, and mountains—the valleys rich and beautiful—the hills covered with tall pines, redwood, and cedar that have withstood the tempests and whirlwinds of a century, and the mountains rising in majestic grandeur to the clouds. In passing out, the valley of San Jose opens to the view in all the loveliness of the climate of Italy and beauty of the tropics. This valley is about sixty miles in length, and ten in width. The Pueblo, which means an incorporated town, is the principal place of business for the valley, and is about five miles from Santa Clara, the landing on the bay, or as it is termed here, "the embarcadero." Passing on from here north east, the traveller in a few hours ride reaches the Straits, which separate the Suisun bay, formed by the confluence of the Sacramento and San Joaquin Rivers, from that of San Pablo. Here it seems that the accumulated waters of a thousand years had suddenly rent the opposing mountain asunder and flowed with tremendous force to the great bosom of the deep.

On the north side of the bay to the straits to Sousilito, is one of the finest districts of country in all upper California.

Next to Yerba Buena, Sousilito is the best point on the whole bay for a commercial town. It is seven miles a little east of north from this place on the opposite side of the bay, and has long been a watering place for vessels.

An attempt has recently been made to lay off and build up a town at the straits to supercede the two last mentioned places. It will no doubt, however, be an entire failure.

San Francisco bay being the safest and most commodious harbor on the entire coast of the Pacific, some point on it must be the great mart of the western world. We believe Yerba Buena is the point, commanding as it does now, all the trade of the surrounding country, and there being already a large amount of capital concentrated here.

The town of Yerba Buena is called in some of the old maps of the country San Francisco. It is not known by that name here, however.

The town takes its name from an herb to be found all around it which is said to make good tea; and possessing excellent medicinal qualities, it is called good herb or Yerba Buena.

Public Meeting (February 20)

A large and respectable public meeting of the citizens of Yerba Buena was held on Monday evening last, on the corner of the Portsmouth Square opposite the Portsmouth House for the purpose of taking into consideration a proper disposition of the public beach lands in front of the town. In answer to a call from a number of citizens we explained the object of the meeting, and offered the following resolution.

Resolved—That we will use every effort to induce the governor and council to divide the beach lands in front of the town into convenient business lots, and to sell them for the benefit of the town, or the Territorial government.

We made a few remarks in support of the resolution, in which we alluded to the attempt of a few designing individuals to appropriate the whole of this valuable property to their use for purposes of speculation. When we concluded, PARSON Dunleavy rose and commenced a heated personal attack upon us. He did not touch the subject before the people, and wound up with an attempt to break up the meeting in a row. We replied in a speech of about an hours length knocking the BARK from him at every word. In our concluding remarks we told him we were sorry that he had put himself forward as the mouth-piece of a NASTY LITTLE CLIQUE. He attempted to reply but was hissed down. Geo. Hyde Esq. then rose and enquired whether he was included among the "nasty little clique."—We remarked that he knew probably better than we did, and if the cap fit, that he might wear it. Several persons in the meeting said at the same time, that they did not know whether the clique was nasty or not, but they knew Mr. Hyde was a d——d dirty fellow. Mr. Hyde enquired the names of the persons who made these remarks—one name was given, whereupon he expressed himself satisfied. After some further discussion the resolution was passed almost unanimously, notwithstanding the strenuous effort on the part of Messrs. W. A. Bartlett, Dunleavy and George Hyde, who made repeated attempts to break up the meeting.

Our Town, Its Prospects (March 13)

The town of Yerba Buena is now rapidly improving, and bids fair to rival in rapidity of progress the most thriving town or city on the American continent. If the necessary labor and lumber can be obtained, from three to five hundred houses will probably go up in the course of the present year. There is room here for artizans, mechanics, and laborers of all kinds. The highest wages are paid, and will continue to be paid; and the highest price for lumber, brick, adobies and every description of building materials, will be given upon their delivery here, payable in cash.

The town of Yerba Buena is no doubt destined to be the Liverpool or New York of the Pacific Ocean. At this point will be concentrated nearly all the commercial enterprize and capital engaged in the Pacific trade. The position of the town for commerce is unrivaled, and never can be rivaled unless some great convulsion of nature shall produce a new harbor on the Pacific coast equalling in beauty and security our magnificent bay. Without difficulty or danger, ships of any burthen can at all times enter the harbor, which is capacious enough to contain the navies of the whole world. The extensive and fertile countries watered by the Sacramento and San Joaquin Rivers, and the numerous navigable creeks emptying into the bay, must, when they are settled upon with an industrious population, as they soon will be, pour their produce into this place, and receive in exchange from our merchants all their supplies of manufactures and luxuries. All the products of the gold, silver, copper, iron, and quicksilver mines, with which the country abounds, must be concentrated here for manufacture and exportation. In a few years, our wharves and streets will present a scene of busy life, resembling those witnessed in Liverpool, New Orleans, and New York. Mechanics and artizans from all parts of the world will flock here, and we shall be in the full enjoyment of all the elegancies and luxuries of the oldest and most polished countries of the globe. This is no fancy sketch; but on the contrary, all who now read, may live to see it fully verified.

The Name of our Town (March 20)

Our readers will perceive that in our present number we have con-
formed to the change recently made in the name of our town, by placing at
the head of our paper SAN FRANCISCO instead of YERBA BUENA. The change
has now been made legally, and we acquiesce in it, though we prefer the
old name—the one by which the place has always been known in this
country. When the change was first attempted, we viewed it as a mere
assumption of authority, without law or precedent, and therefore adhered
to the old name of Yerba Buena. It was asserted by the late Alcalde,
Washington A. Bartlett, that the place was called San Francisco in some old
Spanish paper, which he professed to have in his possession; but how
could we believe a man EVEN about that which it is said "there is nothing
in" who had so often evinced a total disregard for his own honor and
character—the honor and character of the country which gave him birth,
and the rights of his fellow citizens in this distant land? We could not! We
have no confidence in a man who, clothed with a "little brief authority"
oppresses his fellow creatures, and uses the power in his hands to deprive
them of their rights. We have no confidence in a man who suffers himself
to be bribed with a bottle of champagne or a roast turkey; or who as Judge
stains the sacred ermine of the Bench by the reception of a paltry favor,
knowing it to be intended to influence his decision in a case at the time
pending before him. We refrain at present from saying anything further
concerning the mal-practises of the late Alcalde, as we intend in a short
time to expose the whole in one article and publish documentary proof to
sustain every assertion.

Our Town (April 17)

The town of San Francisco is progressing with a rapidity almost without
example, certainly with no example on the waters of the Pacific Ocean. Not
less than fifty houses have gone up within the last month. Every man now
here finds constant employment, and if thousands more were here in
search of labor, they would find it, and receive for their services as much
as any reasonable man would require.

Lumber, adobies, brick and lime, are much wanted, and whoever em-
barks largely in the manufactory of these building materials, for consumption at this place, will reap a rich harvest of profits. The high price now
demanded for them renders building expensive; and the houses now
going up are consequently small. But another year, we trust, will remedy
this difficulty. Unless those who have the control of lumber, and other

building materials here, shall see fit to furnish them at fair rates, they will find ready made houses coming out here in ships, from the states, and that speedily.

Numerous merchant vessels are arriving here almost daily, furnishing our wholesale and retail commercial houses with large supplies of merchandize of every description. San Francisco is now a point where many articles of merchandize can be furnished nearly as cheap as they can be in the United States, carriage and commissions excepted. Merchants along the sea-board to the south can do better by coming here to replenish their stock of merchandize than by sending to the Islands.

"BLOWING UP" THE WIND
by E. C. K.[1] (April 24)

Ever blowing, colder growing, sweeping madly through
    the Town,
Never ceasing, ever teasing, never pleasing, never down.
       Day or night, dark or light,
       Sands a-flying, clapboards sighing—
       Groaning, moaning, whistling shrill,
       Shrieking wild, and never still.
In September, in November, or December, ever so;
E'en in August will the raw gust, flying fine dust,
    roughly blow.
       Doors are slamming, gates a-banging,
       Shingles shivering, casements quivering—
       Roaring, pouring, madly yelling,
       Tales of storm and shipwreck telling.
In our Bay, too, vessels lay-to, find no shelter from
    the blast;
"White caps" clashing, bright spray splashing, light
    foam flashing—dashing past.
       Yards are creaking, "blocks" a-squeaking,
       Rudder rattling, ropes all clattering,
       Lugging, tugging at the anchor,
       Groaning spars and restless "spanker."
Now the sun gleams, bright the day seems—hark!

---

1. Edward C. Kemble.

he comes—is heard the roar.
Haste to dwelling, dread impelling, heap the fire,
    close the door.
        Onward coming, humming, drumming,
        Groaning, moaning, sighing, crying,
        Shrieking, squeaking,—(Reader, 'tis so,)
        Thus bloweth the wind at—

SAN FRANCISCO.

April 20, 1847.

Statistics of San Francisco (August 28)

The town of San Francisco, (*Yerba Buena,*) is situated on the west side of the great Bay of the same name, and on the northern point of the peninsula which lies between the southern portion of the Bay and the Pacific Ocean. It is about four miles from the narrows or straits by which you enter the Bay from the sea. The immediate site of the present town is an indentation or cove in the western shore of the Bay, directly in front of which, and at the distance of about two miles, lies a large island called *Yerba Buena* Island.

From the water's edge the land rises gradually for more than half a mile to the west and southwest, until it terminates in a range of hills of five hundred feet in height at the back of the town. To the north of the town is an immense bluff, (or rather, *three in one,*) more than five hundred feet high, which comes down to the water's edge with precipitous sides of from twenty to one hundred feet in height. In front of this bluff is the best anchorage ground, the bottom being good and the high land protecting shipping from the full blast of the westerly winds which prevail so constantly during the summer season. Between this bluff and the hills above mentioned there is a small and nearly level valley which connects with a smaller cove about a mile nearer the ocean. The bluff forms the northwestern boundary of the cove, and the eastern boundary is another bluff called the *Rincon,* but of only about fifty feet in height. To the south and southwest of this last mentioned point, there is a succession of low sand hills covered with a dense growth of shrubby trees peculiar to the country.

The town plot as recently laid out and surveyed by Mr. Jasper O'Farrell, fronts upon the cove, taking in the high bluff before mentioned and the *Rincon,* and extending about three quarters of a mile from north to south, and two miles from east to west, thus embracing about one and a half square miles. From the water the streets run to the top of the range of hills in the rear of the town, and these streets are crossed at right angles by others running parallel to the water. The squares thus formed are divided into lots of three different sizes, viz:

1st. *Beach and water lots.* The lots comprised in this designation are those situated between high and low water mark. They are sixteen and a half varas in width of front, and fifty varas deep. These lots were surveyed and offered for sale at public auction by order of Gen. Kearny when he was governor of the Territory. There are about four hundred and fifty of them, of which about two hundred were disposed of at the sale in July. They brought prices ranging from fifty dollars to six hundred dollars. . . . About four-fifths of these lots are entirely under water at flood tide, and will therefore require much improvement before they can yield a revenue to the holders; still, they are beyond question the most valuable property in the town.

2d. *Fifty vara lots.* The principal part of the town is laid out in lots of this class. They are of fifty varas depth and front, and six of them make a square. There are now surveyed about seven hundred of this description, of which number four hundred, or perhaps four hundred and fifty, have been sold. These lots are sold at private sale by the *Alcalde* at a fixed price for each. The price established by law is $12 for the lot, to which is to be added the office fees for deed and recording, $3.62½, making in all $15.62½. The conditions of sale are, that the purchaser shall fence the lot and build a house upon it within one year from the day of purchase. If he fail to do this, the lot and improvements revert to the town.

3d. *One hundred vara lots.* The eastern portion of the town is laid out in lots one hundred varas square. This is the largest class, and embraces that part of the town plot which will probably be the last to be improved by purchasers. There are about one hundred and thirty lots of this size, and probably sixty of these are still unsold. These are also disposed of by the *Alcalde* at private sale, at $25 per lot. . . . The conditions of sale are the same as for the fifty vara lots. The sales of both classes are only for cash at the time of the purchase. . . .

The streets in the oldest part of the town are only about sixty feet in width. Those in the more recent surveys are seventy-five and eighty, with one broad Avenue one hundred and ten feet wide. It is a source of regret that any streets should have been less than eighty feet in width.

. . . Permit me to lay before your readers some statistics relative to the number and character of the population who compose the new village, but eventual city, of San Francisco. They were collected in the latter part of June, 1847. . . .

White males–247; females–128. Indian males–26; females–8. Sandwich

Islander males–39; females–1. Negro males–9; females–1. Thus, a total population of 459.

I have no very satisfactory means of judging of the increase of population within the year last past, but the facts I possess render it certain that the increase has been at least one hundred per cent. Of course, the whole of the increase was by emigration.

To form a correct idea of the energy, enterprise, and capability of the white inhabitants, the reader should not fail to note that . . . more than four-fifths are less than forty years of age, and more than one half are between the ages of twenty and forty.

Of the number born in California (38), eight are children of emigrant parents. The others are Californians proper, and they, with two born in other Departments of Mexico, constitute the entire Mexican population. Of the whole number, three-fifths are from the United States. Not only is this true, but probably at least another fifth, including Scotch, Irish, and German emigrants, have reached this country after residing for a time in the United States.

Of the white population, the number who can read and write is 273; who can read but not write is 13; who cannot read or write is 80. From this it appears that the number who cannot read or write bears a very close relation to the number of inhabitants under ten years of age. A fact not to be wondered at when we reflect that there is but one school teacher in the place, and that the town has as yet failed to erect a building suitable for the purposes of education.

The occupations or professions of the white males are as follows:

Ministers	1	Gunsmiths	2
Doctors	3	Hotel keepers	3
Lawyers	3	Laborers	20
Surveyors	2	Masons	4
School Teachers	1	Merchants	11
Agriculturists	11	Miners	1
Bakers	7	Morocco case makers	1
Blacksmiths	6	Navigators (inland)	6
Brewers	1	" (ocean)	1
Brickmakers	6	Painters	1
Butchers	7	Printers	6
Cabinet makers	2	Saddlers	1
Carpenters	26	Shoemakers	4
Cigar makers	1	Silversmiths	1
Clerks	13	Tailors	4
Coopers	3	Tanners	2
Gardeners	1	Watchmakers	1
Grocers	5	Weavers	1

The Indians, Sandwich Islanders, and Negroes, who compose nearly one-fifth of the whole population of the town, are mostly employed as servants and porters. Some of the Indians are very expert in the manufacture of sun dried bricks, (*adobes*) and in the erection of houses from them. The Sandwich Islanders are mostly employed as boatmen in navigating the Bay, and they are said to be very serviceable in the business. Some few of the Sandwich Islanders read, and two or three can both read and write their own language. Occasionally there will an Indian be found who had been learned during the existence of the Missions to read, but such instances are rare. They are, for the most part, an idle, intemperate race, laboring only to procure the means for gratifying their passion for rum and *monte*. Some of the Indians are considered by persons having them as their property, and I am told, though I have never known of such a case, that there have been instances of the sale and transfer of them from one person to another. As there is no necessity for such an institution as slavery in this country, and as most of the emigrants who come here are educated to respect every human being's rights, there can be no doubt that such practices, if they ever did exist, will soon become obsolete. The few Negroes who reside here are from the United States, and are as intelligent as is usual among the free Negroes of the north.

The following statement of the number of offices and places of business is submitted, viz:

Apothecary shops	1	Gunsmith's shops	1
Bakeries	3	Hotels	2
Blacksmith shops	2	Mills (horsepower)	1
Butcher shops	3	" (wind)	1
Cabinet maker's shops	1	Printing offices	2
Carpenter's shops	2	Shoemaker's shops	1
Cigar maker's shops	1	Stores	8
Cooper shops	2	Tailor shops	2
Groceries	7	Watchmaker's shops	1

During the year elapsed previous to the thirtieth of June, 1847, there were built in the town *thirty* houses. Most of these structures are indeed but poor affairs, yet they constitute an important item when taken as an index of the enterprise and improvement which the town exhibits. Since June, and up to the present time, there have been built, (or are in process of erection) at least *twenty* houses. There can be no better evidence of the rapid improvement of the place than this single fact.

CORRECTION (September 4)

In my communication last week on the "Statistics of San Francisco," I stated that there had been at *least twenty houses* built in the town in the two months of July and August. I find, on examination, I have unintentionally done great injustice to the spirit of improvement and progress which pervades the place; for, instead of there having been "at least *twenty*," there were *forty-eight* buildings erected within the time spoken of above.

In the years previous to the first of April 1847, there were erected,

Shanties	22
Frame buildings	31
Adobe buildings	26

Since the first of April, and up to the present time (August 31, 1847,) there have been built, (or are in process of erection.)

Shanties	20
Frame buildings	47
Adobe buildings	11

This shows the astonishing increase within the last *five months* of *one hundred per cent*.

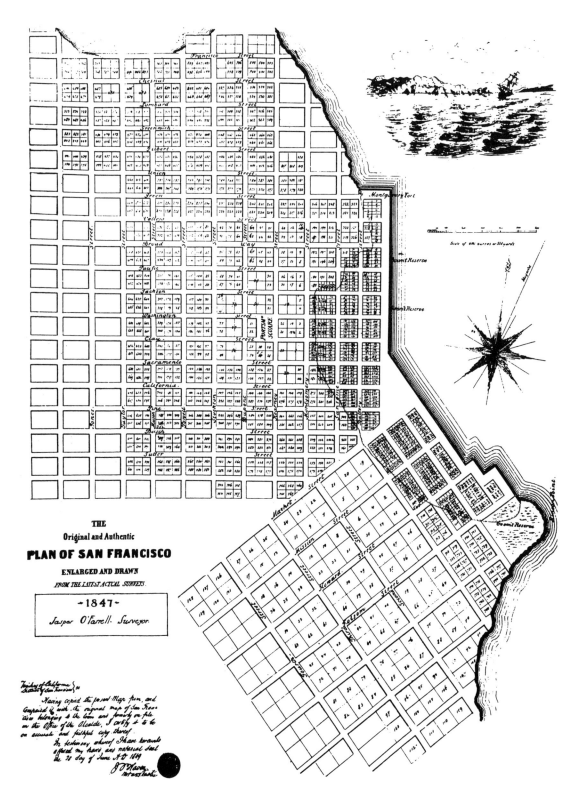

The Original and Authentic Plan of San Francisco, 1847,
by Jasper O'Farrell.

A friend has placed in our possession a copy of the *Revue des Deux Mondes* for January, 1850, containing an article by Consul Dillon on California, as he saw it in September, 1849, the article bearing date Oct. 2d of that year. The *Revue* is a very able quarterly, and the leading literary periodical of France. Mr. Dillon is in such a position before the public, and has such a reputation, that all his words and deeds, particularly those in regard to America, may be considered as having a kind of general interest, and part of what he wrote of California in 1849 deserves to be read for itself alone. Mr. Dillon's labors have not all been confined to the diplomatic line; for he has done something also as a *litterateur*. (From the San Francisco *Daily California Chronicle*, August 25, 1855.)

California in September 1849

Patrice Dillon
from the *Revue des Deux Mondes*

Yerba Buena, alias San Francisco, lies upon the right of the entrance of the Bay of San Francisco a short distance beyond the old Spanish fort. It is today a city of 50,000 souls, and promises to be in a short time the metropolis of the Pacific Ocean. Dense forests of masts, extending far on all sides, recall Havre and Marseilles. There are now more than three hundred and forty merchant ships at anchor in the harbor, without counting a large number of brigs and schooners. All, without exception, have lost their crews, and from many the captains themselves have deserted. An American sloop-of-war, bearing the flag of Commodore Jones, is the only guard of these vessels.

We disembarked without difficulty on a wharf hastily constructed near the ancient fort. Here there are no custom-house officers to stick their fingers in your pockets, or to turn your trunks and packages upside down. The interior customs, (taxes,) that intolerable scourge, are unknown among the Americans. Time for them has a value equivalent to money; and everything which takes away their time without an evident necessity, is considered as an infringement on their liberties. True liberty, in the eyes of an American, consists not in arguing for extravagant theories to a rabid audience, but in the privilege of devoting himself, without any hindrance, to the occupations which suit his taste.

At San Francisco, fifteen months ago, there were only half a dozen rude cabins, and now there is a Merchants' Exchange, a theatre, churches for all forms of Christian worship, and a large number of neat houses. Some of them are of stone, but the greater number of them are of wood or adobes. The house fronts are painted or white-washed; the streets are straight; and the city presents a very respectable appearance. On two sides of the city following the shore, there are rows of tents extending as far as the eye can reach, making a new city, not without its features of originality. There, previous to starting for the mines, the immigrants from the two hemispheres go to repose for a short time before starting out. There are Chinese, Malays, Botany Bay convicts, and wanderers and outcasts from all the islands of the Pacific. There is King Kamehameha's former Minister of Justice, now the most redoubtable brigand of California, the author of that famous code of laws which the Bible societies of England and America pronounced a master-piece of human wisdom. There are assassins, thieves, highway robbers, and buccaneers upon whom the hand of justice has not yet fallen. There might be found rich and abundant materials for comedy and tragedy. There can be heard the particulars of miraculous escapes and wonderful adventures, wilder than any dreamed of by our wildest romancers.

Already the city of San Francisco resembles a vast hive, in which there is a fierce humming. Carriages, wagons, carts and drays fly pell-mell in all directions. I pity the philosopher, the dreamer who may find himself strayed away in the streets of this city, for at every moment when he may fall into meditation he incurs the risk of being run over without the satisfaction of having been told to "look out." Great teamsters, of large and bony frames, wearing sugar-loaf hats, lash their horses through the streets without any regard to footmen. On all sides is to be seen a silent and preoccupied crowd, hurrying along, either towards the Custom House—a rude building near the lower end of the city—or to the Merchants' Exchange, which has gambling houses on each side, and in front groups of eager speculators.

All the nations of the globe are largely represented in the commerce of San Francisco; but as might be expected, the American element is dominant. The American laws permit every one to follow such occupation as pleases him, and consequently every body is a broker, consignee, banker, or commission merchant, and some perform the function of all of these at once. I do not know whether the shippers and exporters of Havre sending goods to San Francisco make their fortunes; but I do know that the consignees are not ruined. The sum of their various commissions for sale, exchange, storage, etc., would greatly edify the commission merchants of Europe. The total per centage on sales may be stated at 50 per cent without exaggeration. But the consignee in San Francisco has heavy expenses to pay. An egg costs five francs, a potatoe sometimes three, and the rents vary from $30,000 to $10,000 per year. There are houses in considerable number which pay a rent of $140,000 per year.

Great as may be the produce of the mines of California, and however numerous the resources of San Francisco as a centre of commerce, it is

The Port of San Francisco, June 1, 1849, by George H. Baker.
The view is from Rincon Hill, looking northwest, showing the embryo city flanked by Russian and Telegraph hills, with Mt. Tamalpais, Angel Island, and the hills of Marin in the distance.

impossible that the present state of affairs should long continue. The Yankee is a born speculator; nobody understands the nature of a puff better than he. Give a hundred acres of marsh to a New Englander, and he will baptize it "Eden Fields," and then he will place a high valuation on it, in so many different manners and with so much perseverance, that some "innocent" body will soon fall into the trap. This, in the United States, is styled to "play a Yankee trick," (*jouer un tour de Yankee,*) and certainly Gen. Jackson was not more proud of his famous victory at New Orleans, than one of these successful speculators, when he recounts, to enthusiastic compatriots, some successful adventure of this nature. Throw three Americans on a desert island, where there is only one spring of fresh water, and two of them will squat on it, and make the other pay for his water; and then they will brag of the Yankee trick.

The great number of gambling houses gives, at present, a factitious and exaggerated value to the real estate in San Francisco. All the exiles from Frascati, from Nos. 36 and 113 of the Palace Royal, and from the similar establishments of London, Berlin, and Vienna, appear to have collected in this, the promised land of gamblers. The moment that a house is offered to let, the gamblers take possession of it, and the bank, with its appurtenances, is opened. There are more than a hundred of these houses now in this city, where a multitude of vagabonds and adventurers from the Sandwich Islands, Malay-dom, China, and the rest of the world, crowd and elbow each other every night. All the nations of the earth have poured their scum into this sewer of humanity.

There is no sight more wonderful than is to be seen in the gambling houses every evening. Outside, a dense crowd obstructs the door. Inside, men, eager to bet, force a passage to the Monte-table, and, in their excitement, often get to fighting. Elsewhere, quarrels of such a kind would be settled with the fist. But, in California, an injury, or even a slight touch sometimes, is followed forthwith by an attack with a pistol or knife. When a banker hears a pistol shot in the room he cries out, "Silence, down there; you d——d rascals make too much noise." If the disorder continue, another banker will cry, "I'll make a hole in you; the devil take me if I don't." Such are the short but significant expressions heard on all sides. When the new comer—generally from the mines—gets before the gambling table, he takes off a buckskin belt, and shakes out some chunks of gold upon the table. The "head manager" takes them, weighs them upon a pair of scales at his side, and pays him for the dust in gold ounces, at $16 each. The game is made, the gambler collects the bets, and, at the end of twenty minutes, the miner has to take off his belt again, and pour out more dust. It often happens that, in one night, a miner is relieved of all his superfluous gold.

I have just returned from dining with one of the most successful speculators of the city. He is an American, a bankrupt merchant, who arrived in California six months ago, and is now worth $200,000. Among the guests were several officers of the Unites States Army and Navy. The dinner was prolonged till a late hour, and seasoned with toasts and speeches. On leaving the house, one of the officers proposed to serve me as a cicerone. I accepted the offer. We went to one of the largest gambling houses. Arrived at the green-table, not without effort, I threw down a dollar, without hope. A young man with a long beard, and grave and aristocratic manners, presided. He stopped a moment to look at me, and, pushing my piece back, said, in good French, "I see that Monsieur is a stranger, and ignorant of our usages. Here we do not play for five-franc pieces, but for ounces. Please to take back your hundred cents;" placing a slight accent on the last words. Struck with the man's manners, I waited for a favorable occasion to get into conversation with him, and he was very polite. "You wish," said he, "to know whether our bank does a good business. I will be candid with you. We have been doing pretty well, except that, to-night, business is detestable. In the last eight hours our profits have not been more than $20,000. Fortunately, we have done better on other evenings; for $20,000 profit in a night is a poor affair in this country." My informant then told me that he had played an important part in one of the clubs of Paris, until the events of June 1848. "We lost the game there," said he, "and, therefore, I sought another theatre."

The passion for play has not been imported into California by the Americans. The natives of California were always great gamblers, and in Mexico the same taste prevails. The favorite game is monte; but roulette has its partizans likewise, as well as a game styled "the beasts" (des betes,) in which figures of animals placed at the end of a capstan, furnished with moveable rings, receive a rotary impulse, and stop opposite to a certain apartment containing the figures of animals.

The population of San Francisco increases every day with immigrants by sea from all parts of the world. The Sandwich Islands, Tahiti, the Viti and Feejee Islands, New Zealand, and Sydney, are emptied more or less of their white population. All these heterogeneous elements have come to dissolve themselves in the great mass of workers. Now absent, the emigrants will return at the beginning of winter to seek the shelter of the city. The present population is composed only of the traders, ship captains, and those who, having collected money in the mines, are here to spend it in gambling or debauch. The population is almost entirely male, and the few respectable women scarcely dare to venture into the streets. Nevertheless, a notable improvement has taken place since the pure American element has the predominance. Now nobody can insult a woman with impunity. It is well known that in no place is woman more respected than in the United States. For the rest, occupations under the ban of public opinion in Europe are here in a flourishing condition, and scarcely a week passes without the arrival of some American or Chilean vessel with a feminine cargo, shipped by speculators. This trade, as I am assured, is now the most profitable of all.

The rarity of thefts in San Francisco, notwithstanding the facilities of every kind offered to the evil instincts of the suspected population, is surprising. Thus, in the yards of the private houses, in the streets, or the public squares, and at every turn, one rubs against piles of merchandise from all parts of the globe, and scattered about apparently without protection, and yet the professional rouges do not touch them. The reason is, that California, like every other country, has its own peculiar code of morality—a code accepted and recognized by all. Thus the caprice of using a knife or a pistol in a fight can be overlooked, but to touch the property of another person is the greatest of enormities. A score of balls will fly from the surrounding tents at the thief if he is detected. Merchant, miner, boatmen, every body will quit his occupation to pursue the offender, for every body is interested to prevent theft. And yet there is no soldiery nor police to look after the public interests. Such a condition of things would, in Europe, excite astonishment and indignation. People there could not conceive that a government should so neglect its most essential duty as to grant no official and direct protection to a country under its flag, but many things inconceivable to the European are simple and natural to the American. Society, according to his ideas, is only a union of intelligent and free elements, each part of which is drawn by a peculiar affinity to its natural position. The intervention of the civil power, except in a case of extreme need, would only derange this tendency, and interfere with the natural gravitation. It is better that each individual should do his share in repressing social disorder, than to abandon the matter to the State, and thus place the people under a sort of guardianship. Let us not pity the Americans too much for being thus constituted. If we wish in Europe to admit the people to share in political power, it will be necessary for us to learn, like the Americans, to expect much from ourselves and little from the government, to moderate and govern the excitement inseparable from any large participation of the people in governmental affairs. When the rich middle class first claimed the right—apparently extravagant—of sharing all the privileges of the nobility, the latter was greatly alarmed. They exclaimed that society was menaced by anarchy and chaos. Little by little, the nobility took up the new movement, then directed it, and even turned it to their own advantage. It is necessary for the middle classes to imitate the example of the nobility. There is only one method of escaping the dangers of democracy—and that is, to elevate the masses, to make common cause with them, and to descend boldly into the arena of politics whenever the public tranquility is menaced.

The most perfect tranquility reigns now in the mines. Frenchmen, Americans, Englishmen work side by side in peace. The presence of a pick or a pan in the vicinity of a mining claim shows that it is private property. Upon seeing this sign, the miners pass on to seek for unoccupied ground. Often rumors circulate of rich diggings in this or that place; a crowd collects; but the new comers respect the early claims, and are content to settle in the vicinity of the discoverers.

The gold-seeker is not a socialist, though a democrat. He consents that you should keep the hole which you have made, but he will make a violent resistance if you claim a whole valley or flat. It is partly because the Mexicans and Chileans have worked in large gangs for speculators and not directly for themselves, that the Americans have in some places risen and driven them from the mines. It is true that the quarrel ended by a feud between the two races. Bands of Americans, principally from Oregon, even wished to expel all who did not speak English. There was a time when the French were seriously menaced. They armed themselves and sent a deputy to see the Americans. This happened just when the latter were making preparations to celebrate the 4th of July. The deputy gave notice of the desire of the French to avoid a difficulty, but of the intent to fight rather than to be driven off. Some of the Americans were in favor of battle, but the great majority were for peace. An orator cried "Why fight with the French? Their fathers were the friends of our fathers. They fought together for the same cause, the independence of our country, and against the same enemy, the English. Rochambeau was a Frenchman; so was Lafayette. They are heroes in our history, and their names rank in the memory of every true American by the side of that of Washington. To-day is the anniversary of our independence; we will unite in a banquet to celebrate it. The French have a place naturally at the table; let us send a delegation to invite them to it."

This address was received with long cheers, and in the evening the two races were united about the same table and fraternized uproariously. From that moment the French and Americans have been on the most friendly terms. And here I cannot resist the temptation to render homage to the noble characters of the Americans of the West—that simple-hearted but loyal and energetic position of a great people. I have often met these bold children of the forests and the solitudes; I have exchanged with them, on more than one perilous occasion, warm hand-grasps, and ardent felicitations. Frenchmen [!] at heart and true friends of liberty, they rejoice with a deep joy at all the good fortune of their great ally, as they still style France. For the men of the West, for the American tillers of the soil, the epoch of the Revolutionary War is the heroic age of their country. There is not one of them who is not thoroughly acquainted with the events of that great struggle—who does not remember and venerate the names of all who figured in it. As to the events of their history, since that time, they have only a vague idea of it, and pay little attention to it. If at times the American policy is hostile to France it is because the great West forgets to raise her voice.

The French are, next to the Americans, the most numerous portion of the population of California, and number about 10,000. Those among them who conduct themselves well—and I am happy to say the large majority do so—succeed very well. More sober than the Americans and the English, they escape many excesses to which the others are given. But here, as

Custom House on the Plaza
(From *The Annals of San Francisco.*)

elsewhere, fortune remains with the man who expends little, rather than with him who gains much. I see merchants who are said to have done an extensive business, and yet are embarrassed in their affairs; while many others, who have been dealing along prosaically, have become wealthy. For the American, as for the English merchant, pleasure is incompatible with business. They act like champions who had entered an arena on which they were to have a mortal struggle. There is no repose, no amusement for them. To come as conquerors from the scene, to surpass all rivals—that is the end of all their desires, the glorious result to be attained by their efforts.

I have often stopped in San Francisco before the shops and stands of the young men from New York, just out of school, as yet beardless, who act the salesman with an address which would put the best clerk of Paris to the blush. Look at the play of the countenance of that young merchant; observe the choice of his words, the vivacity and the naturalness of his gesticulation; he is not offering to you a pocket handkerchief, or a pair of pantaloons, or a box of sardines—no, it is the philosopher's stone with which he will part to you, only out of pure love for humanity. Excellent young man!—how often have I admired your precocious eloquence and your imperturbable self-possession. You will make your fortune.

The perseverance of the American trader is not one of the least causes of the immense development of the commerce of the United States in the last few years. These men consider it patriotic to attempt to crush the rival industry of all other nations, while they push forward their own. "Have you read the last report of Collector King?" an American will say to you as he catches you by the button hole, while satisfaction is perceptible in all his features. "Read it; you will see that we are about to overthrow John Bull. The tonnage of our mercantile marine almost equaled his last year; this year we will ride over him. We have chased his calicoes from Brazil; we shall certainly soon expel them from China. Is not that glorious?" On hearing such words, so full of a strange enthusiasm, I cast a look at France, where, alas! like the Greeks of the Lower Empire, we are quarreling about philosophic or political formulas, while the two great nations which alone march side by side with us in the world of ideas and of facts, extend and develop their influence and their commerce throughout the earth. When will the genius of France—that genius once so active and fecund—desert the war which can lead only to anarchy? When will France return to the track of practical and material reform? France, whose intellectual wealth has enriched all about her—when will she see that, in attempting to realize chimerical theories, she must incur the risk of being reduced, like Niobe, to weep among the tombs?

On May 30 and 31, 1856, the San Francisco *Daily California Chronicle* reprinted articles from the *Yreka Union*. The writer, an unidentified single man, had arrived in California in November 1849 via the Lassen route after crossing the plains. He wrote of his journey down into the Sacramento Valley, and continued by describing his experiences and misadventures when he encountered the new California culture.

Scenes in California in 1849

By a young man of no means, but wits

Next day I arrived at the little place or ranch called Nicholas,[1] where quite a crowd was collected. The charge to lie on the floor was $1; meals, $2; drinks, 60 cents. I took out a handsome silk handkerchief which I had preserved from the time I left Independence; and although it was a present from a favorite of mine, I offered it for my supper and privilege to sleep under the roof. It was granted; and the next morning I had breakfast and my handkerchief returned to me.

At this place everything seemed to be in confusion—Colt's revolvers, knives, &c., lying about the place. The miners of those days, however, dreaded little of losing by thieves; Lynch law was the supreme power, and put into execution for a trifling cause. I started again on my way for Sacramento, not feeling inclined to go to the mines, particularly as I thought there would be more chance of getting plenty to eat in a city. Next day I came to quite a little town called Vernon, opposite Fremont, on the Sacramento river.[2] Every one here was busy—some at work putting up buildings, and others fencing in lots. I looked about to discover someone I might know, but they were all strangers to me. I felt hungry, and, taking courage, went into a store and asked for some hard bread, saying that I had no money. I got plenty of bread and some drink; the store belonged to Col. Grant. On the opposite side of the street was a large building, a hotel, kept by Capt. Savage. I walked over to it; the owner was standing at the door,

---

1. A ranch and trading post operated by Nicolaus Allgeier, on the east side of the Feather River some eighteen miles below Yuba City.
2. These two upstart towns were at the juncture of the Feather and Sacramento rivers. They both vanished, but Vernon was reborn as Verona about 1906—it couldn't have its original name because there was by then a town in another county with that name.

and I inquired of him what men were getting a day to hire out. He said from $8 to $10. I replied that I would be glad to take the half of it, provided the work was not too hard. He said he would give me work that would suit me, and that I should have $5 a day and found—to be ready in the morning to go in the boat down the river, where he had a number of men employed pressing hay; hay at this time was worth $100 a ton.

About ten o'clock the little steamboat started, the captain having been directed to leave me at the proper place. I was received kindly by the men; they were all Germans, and perfect gentlemen. One of them at the present day is the owner of an extensive brewery in Marysville, and another is a well-known merchant of San Francisco. The work just suited me; I had only to rake the hay that had got wet, to dry by the sun. I remained at this place three weeks, and received $72.

Now, having a little cash, I left for Sacramento. The morning I landed at Sacramento, a crowd was collected on the levee around a man who was shouting he had all the latest dates from every part of the States—who wanted to hear from home? He could give them a paper for one dollar. This gentlemen is now an extensive broker in San Francisco (Jo. Grant). Having a natural taste for trading, I thought I could not do better than make a little speculation with the few dollars I had—attracted by a red flag and bell ringing I walked over to an auction that was being held on the street. A lot of Manila cigars were up; six dollars was all that was bid; I cried out the half, and they were knocked down to me. Until I received them, I did not know how many I was to get; I got ten thousand cigars for $6.50—that day and next I remained in Sacramento retailing by the hundred these cigars; I made one hundred and fifty dollars by the speculation.

With nearly two hundred dollars in my pocket, I now felt pretty independent. In the evening, while looking at the sights, I was attracted by music, and went into an elegantly fitted-up tent or canvass saloon—here the eye was dazzled by lights, pictures of Venus, &c. In this room were about twenty tables surrounded by crowds of people, seemingly from every nation on the globe, watching intently the games going on. Curiosity induced me to go over to one of them; I saw, as I thought, the dead chance of making a small pile. The gambler said he would not bet under two hundred dollars. An honest looking fellow by my side said he would bet fifty dollars, all he had; but the gambler refused to take so small a sum. I thought there was now a good chance for me to double my money—surely, the young man near me would not risk fifty dollars, unless he was sure of winning. Excited by the chance I saw before me of making money so easy, I whispered to the young man near me that I would put in the one hundred and fifty with him; the bet was made. I put forward my hand, took up the card turned up a little in the corner, which I should have taken my oath was the jack—but discovered too late I was tricked—it was the king! It was not long after this I learned the nice young gentleman was a partner in the game. I left the saloon that night, promising myself never to be caught again in gambling. I got disgusted with Sacramento, and determined to leave for San Francisco as soon as possible.

The next morning I went on board the steamer *McKim,* bound for San Francisco—passage $30. The *McKim* was a very slow boat, and did not arrive at San Francisco until the next morning. The passengers were landed from a row boat on the present Montgomery street, facing Commercial street. I had but $3 in my pocket. The first place I made for was an eating house. It chanced to be kept by Chinese; I had an excellent dinner for $1. At this time I had not yet heard of stewed rats, &c. The place was crowded, the tables were never empty, all day meals were ready. Chinese waiters attended the customers; in the kitchen I believed there was an American who served out the dishes. When I was dining, three droll fellows sat down; the waiter asked, "What you take, John?" One said, "A plate of mahogany shavings;" another, "A plate of roasted cock-roaches." The waiter cried out to the cook for them, to the great amusement of all in the room. John soon came back, and said, "No shaba them, John."

In San Francisco, at this time, there were only about half a dozen of comfortable looking houses, and they were adobes. The hotels and lodging-houses were made of canvass, or canvass-roofed. I got lodgings in a small canvass house. At one end of it a slip of canvass was put up to divide the ladies' apartment from the men's. Two married ladies stopped here with their husbands. Montgomery street appeared to be the centre of business; the street was filled with merchandise; in some parts benches were along the side walks, covered with every kind of articles—rot-gut, shovels, picks, rockers, guns, pistols, knives, &c. were all to be had here. Most numerous were the coffee and refreshment stands—these establishments did a large business. Men had no time to sit down to a meal. Many of the owners of these establishments have returned to the States with a large pile each. In this street every hour a bell could be heard announcing the auction of merchandise. On one day I saw 4,000 lbs. of good chewing tobacco sold for three cents per lb.—the market was flooded with tobacco. I have seen, where frame buildings were going up, large boxes of tobacco put in the ground to be used as a foundation. It answered the purpose very well, and besides was cheaper than any thing else they could get at the time.

The Plaza in San Francisco, now known as Portsmouth Square, was surrounded with a few shanties and tents, and in all of them gambling was carried on. The "Bella Union" was the grandest; it was fitted out superbly, the walls covered with paintings, some most costly—magnificent chandeliers hanging from the ceiling, dazzling the eyes, large mirrors at the end of the room reflecting the saloon, which made it appear as long again. At this place it was no uncommon circumstance for the owners of the gaming tables to win twenty thousand dollars in a night. Sitting at every table, to attract and allure, were some of the prettiest girls and women that could be procured in San Francisco, and they were well paid by the proprietors for their time. From eight to twelve o'clock in the night this saloon was the most attractive place in the city—it reminded me of a grand fancy ball; those who were not gambling were promenading up and down the room. The best musicians that San Francisco could procure at the time were engaged, and delighted the crowd with their harmony. Americans from Pike county, Missouri, as well as the shrewd Yankee from Maine, Spanish gentlemen, wearing their costly wrappers, by the side of the dark-eyed Senorita smoking her cigarrito, Chileans, Sandwich Islanders, (men and women), French, Italians, Portuguese, English, Canadians, Irish, Scotch, Russians, Germans, Chinese, &c. Not a man was to be seen without a pistol and knife in his belt. Sometimes a respectable looking young man would accost me, inquiring if I would purchase a pistol, watch, knife, &c., that he wanted to raise money to bring him to the mines.

There was one young man in particular who attracted my attention; he must be well remembered by those who were in San Francisco at this time; his arms were loaded with China silk handkerchiefs—he sold them for half a dollar each—his voice was most peculiar when crying aloud—"Only half a dollar each!" He informed me he sold three hundred handkerchiefs in the evening at the Bella Union. He afterwards became an extensive merchant in San Francisco, and left in 1851 with his fortune made. Who can forget seeing the celebrated "Fountain Head" man, with his tray tied round his neck full of the best peppermint and hoarhound candy—only one quarter a stick? Often have I purchased a few cigars from a man in this saloon, who is now one of the most extensive merchants in California. From among the lowest class of traders of that day some of our present richest merchants have sprung. Men who lived in affluence and comfort at home, were glad to get the most menial occupation in San Francisco. The son of one of the richest men in Cincinnati was, to my amazement, lamp cleaner at the Empire House—we traveled together over the plains. Preachers were bar-keepers, judges and doctors were waiters in several of the eating-houses. Mechanics undertook to work at every branch they could get employment at, whether it was their own or not. Generally speaking, those who had lived in luxury at home, were unfitted to work in California, and became so reduced as to become loafers, and backers to gambling tables.

These gentlemen would often try to induce the stranger, after a short acquaintance, to accompany them to a table where they would show him how he could win a few hundred dollars; they have often been successful in taking the last dollar from their dupe. With the exception of this mode of robbery, there was little other practised. The streets, by day and night, were filled with boxes, trunks, merchandise, &c. Murdering and stabbing was the order of the day; scarcely a day but some one was shot or stabbed. Often have I heard the cry, "Don't shoot this way!" and immediately afterwards the report of a pistol, when passing some of those gambling houses. On one occasion a ball passed so close to my arm that my coat was marked by it.

Soon after my arrival in San Francisco I was without a dollar—my last one had gone for payment for my sleeping place. I went into the street and stopped at a coffee stand; I told the proprietor I had no money, and asked if he would credit me for a cup of coffee and a little bread. He refused to let me have them. Soon after I was standing on Montgomery street, feeling very uncomfortable without my breakfast, when a mate of a ship came up and inquired if there were any men about would like a job; I immediately replied that I would like to get some work—he soon made out four others. He told us we would get two dollars an hour for our work. I followed him to a boat which took us along side the vessel—she had arrived the evening before, and immediately afterwards the crew deserted her. We went to work raising the anchor; the only help I believe I gave was by singing for the men, as we went round, for I was still very weak from the effects of the overland journey. After getting up the anchor, the captain said, "Any of the men who would remain on board that day and night to keep watch, he would pay them additional." One young fellow and myself agreed to remain; we had both just arrived by the plains, and neither of us knew much about the sea. We had a good dinner and supper on board.

During the night, when I was on watch, the ship began to roll awfully— I got alarmed, ran down to the Captain's room and called him up. When he came on deck he inquired what I called him for; I asked him if he did not perceive the motion of the ship? He d—d me for disturbing him, and left me again with a volley of curses. Next morning quite a storm arose— the Captain called out to the mate and another man to go and make fast a rope to another vessel. In the meantime I was ordered to pull in a certain rope—I pulled the first one I saw. It was now the Captain became frantic with rage; he walked about the deck cursing me for coming on board—that his vessel would be lost. Shortly after, the mate returned, having made the rope fast to the vessel. I was now paid and sent on shore with seven dollars in my pocket.

Next day, while roaming about the city, I saw about fifty men at work grading a block in Sansome street, near the present Oriental Hotel. I inquired who the boss was—I was told Mr. Bryant, who wrote the "Overland Journey." I waited on him and asked for work—he desired me to be there the next morning. I worked here about six weeks at $5 per day. Among the crowd I was with, there were two of the company I left Independence with, one a doctor, the other a lawyer; a finer lot of men I never beheld; I learned that many of them were professional men, necessity obliging them to work at this time on the public street.

After I had saved up a hundred dollars, I commenced to attend auctions. I was generally fortunate in my purchases. On one occasion I bought six large cases of goods; they were sold "blind"; the auctioneer declared he did not know what they contained; he would not allow them to be opened; they were to be sold to pay storage. I purchased them for $160. Upon opening them, I found they contained hardware of every description—locks, bolts, hinges, &c. I sold them next day to a merchant for $500. At another time I bought ten casks of merchandise for $90; upon examining them, found they contained crucibles, which, at that day, were a drug in the market; they could be picked up about the streets.

San Francisco in 1849, from the head of Clay Street.
(From *The Annals of San Francisco.*)

Leonard Kip (1826–1906) of Albany, New York was one of the many who heeded the siren call of gold and went to California in 1849. He was also one of the considerably smaller number who returned home after seeing the sights and having a fling at gold mining. As did thousands of others, he wrote an account of his experiences and observations: *California Sketches, with Recollections of the Gold Mines*, published in Albany in 1850.

William Antonio Richardson, the first inhabitant of Yerba Buena, initially lived in a tent, which he soon replaced with a crude board shack. In 1837 he built what came to be known as the *casa grande*—a large adobe structure on the west side of Grant (nee Dupont) Street north of Clay. At one time the most prominent building in Yerba Buena, it was gone just three years after the Gold Rush—and Richardson was dead only four years later.

Recollections and Requiem

California Sketches, and The Old Adobe

What a puzzling place it was to comprehend! I sat upon a box at the corner of the street, and was for a time bewildered with the bustle which surrounded me. Wall-street itself never presented a busier aspect. Launches were constantly arriving from the various ships; well filled teams were every moment dropping their freight beside the several stores; a continual stream of active population was winding among the casks and barrels which blocked up the place where the sidewalks ought to have been; and in front, an auctioneer was knocking down goods to a crowd, which every nation helped to compose: principally Americans, but liberally sprinkled with Chinese, Chilians, Negroes, Indians and Kanakas; while the comical conjunction of red shirts, gold epaulettes, Spanish panchoes, long queues and coonskin caps gave it almost a carnival aspect.

At length rising, I strolled up one of the streets to the Plaza, an open place, delightfully studded with provision booths and piles of building materials. On one side was a long low Spanish building, constructed of sun-dried brick, with broad wooden porticoes. It was then performing duty as a custom-house. Near it stood a little wooden fabric of more modern date, in which the Alcalde reigned, the supreme judge of law and order. Opposite was the celebrated Parker House, a two story wooden building, very much resembling the better sort of country residences. Every one has heard of this building, with its enormous rent of $175,000. It is sufficient here to state, that the tenant who paid such a sum made a liberal profit in under-letting the rooms and corners of rooms. Though it was ostensibly a hotel, yet boarding and lodging were but a secondary part of its business. It was from its well filled bar, and from the several rooms appropriated to gambling, that the chief profits were realized.

With the exception of the Custom House, all the buildings which fronted upon the square were of wood, and, in most of them, gambling was the chief business: openly practised, because legalized by the city council. Each building had its name painted conspicuously upon the front; and the El Dorado, Alhambra, Verandah, Bella Union, &c. severally presented their claims for patronage. I peeped into many, and was surprised to see how easily French paper, fine matting, and a small chandelier, can convert the rough ribs of an old barn into an elegant hall. At the end was generally the bar, to and from which a continual stream of thirsty souls was pouring. Along the sides, faro, roulette, and more especially monte, displayed their charms—not unsuccessfully, it would seem, by the crowds with which they were all surrounded. Merchants and laborers, navy officers and sailors, Yankees, Hoosiers, Irish, Mexicans, Chilians, Negroes, Chinese and Sandwich Islanders all united here, and lost their money with singular complacency; and as fast as any left the place, the music of harps and violins continually tempted others in to try their luck.

Leaving these dens, which are open night and day, nor even yield respect to the sabbath, I passed down one of the side streets, an avenue which seemed, by some prescriptive rights, to be dedicated exclusively to restaurants. These were very numerous, and, in many cases, not very cleanly. Many of them had the walls lined with bunks, for the sleeping accommodation of such as had not a store or office in which to pass the night; and one of these berths was furnished at the moderate charge of a dollar. Thus, as a single room contained all the elements of board and lodging, many of the proprietors arrogated for their houses the title of hotels, and accordingly chose the highest sounding names in the scope of their memory. The first one naturally named his place the Astor House; the next displayed the magic name of Delmonico on his sign; then followed a numerous collection of shanty eating houses, dignified by the titles of Irving House, Revere House, St. Charles, American, United States, &c.; until the last comers were very much mortified to find that all the finer names had been monopolized, and that it was necessary to descend to less startling titles.

And now, passing through these gastronomic regions, the houses became more scattered, and the more luxurious tenements of clap-board and shingle gave place to slight frames, covered with canvas or even with calico. At intervals, a snug dwelling had been constructed from some ship's caboose, and in one place, a large packing-box, by the application of plenty of clean straw, had been hastily turned into a pleasant little bedroom, somewhat resembling a kennel to be sure, but not for all that a whit the less comfortable inside.

A few minutes walk, and these gave place to tents, where resided those who were preparing to go to the mines, and choose to board and lodge themselves, in preference to paying the exorbitant charges of the hotels. The several encampments were in three little hollows at the outskirts of the city, named severally, "Happy, Pleasant, and Contented valleys;" probably by poetic license, as the dusty prickly shrubs which grew near, and the heads and horns of slaughtered oxen which lay thickly around, certainly did not tend to make them inviting places for country residences.

The last row of tents, with its accompaniment of kettles and camp-fires at length was passed, and the city lay behind me. I climbed to the top of the nearest hill, and sitting upon the stump of what had once been a flag-staff, saw the surrounding sea and country unfolded for miles away. The city, lying apparently so close below that it seemed as though one could throw a stone within its plaza,—the bay, with its hundreds of ships, which, from my elevation, I could easily count,—the entrance from the sea, up which two vessels were slowly beating;—all these formed a scene of great beauty. And while I gazed toward the ocean, the desire seized me of continuing my walk in that direction, and making a circuit back to the city.

Descending the hill and passing two or three ranchoes, each flanked by a well filled enclosure of cattle, I came to the Praesidio, the old barracks of the country. Mexican soldiers no longer stood sentinel around it, nor indeed, did it at first sight appear habitable. The rains of winter had melted away the clumsy brick in many places, and what had once been a compact range of buildings, enclosing the three sides of a handsome square, now more resembled a detached mass of ugly huts. Some of the rooms were occupied by workmen, and the only signs of war were the few guns and mortars which stood exposed in front. Two of them were long and cumbersome, and emblazoned with the arms of Spain, presenting a marked contrast to the Saxon simplicity of the American pieces beside them.

A mile further, and the wagon ruts upon the turf, insensibly led me to the old fort, which commands the entrance to the bay. Had nature consulted a bevy of army officers before beginning her work, she could scarcely have formed a better location. It is at the narrowest part of the channel, and from the southern side, a circular rock of considerable extent rises over a hundred feet from the water, being connected with the main land by a causeway just wide enough for two wagons to pass. The rock being naturally level on top, a bulwark of adobe brick around the edge was all that had been left for man to construct; and at the expense of a few hundred dollars, the Mexican government had thus built up a battery as stout and impregnable as many a one which had cost millions elsewhere.

From the fort it was a walk of many miles over the country to the old mission of San Francisco. Its former flourishing appearance had departed. Of the many old priests who had spent their lives in a noble object, but one remained; and the influence of strangers had almost counteracted the work which his brothers in the cause had so well performed. The adobe church was falling rapidly into ruins, as well as the few houses which clustered about it. The once beautiful gardens were almost broken up and destroyed, and, of the natives who once had congregated for instruction, but a few remained. Even these lingered, not that they loved the locality, but because all connection with their tribes had long since been broken off, and they had not elsewhere to go.

One thing forced itself upon me in my walk. I had seen much to interest me, but I had met little which could give future prosperity to the country. The soil seemed poorly adapted to cultivation, being but seldom irrigated, and timber was entirely wanting; the only vegetation being a species of scrub bush, unavailable for any useful purpose.

Night had begun to fall as I reentered the city, and, as light after light appeared, I could easily distinguish, in every direction, the drinking and gaming houses crowded with their votaries. There were also a circus, a fancy ball, and a negro concert, each in successful performance. The town seemed running wild after amusement, and the lower the tastes to which any of them pandered the better it was sustained.

But the thing most worthy of attention was a political meeting, which was being held upon the plaza. Orators were in full gesticulation upon a staging, and rudely painted transparencies threw a yellow light upon the surrounding crowd. At the close of every sentence, fierce yells and hurrahs arose, not so much from admiration of the speaker, as from a wish to copy the United States in all things; and when the opposition managed to pull down the staging, the shouts grew louder than ever, and even the party attacked seemed delighted at the success of the imitation. And so closed the day.

THE OLD ADOBE

From the *Daily Alta California*, May 3, 1852

Workmen are now engaged in tearing down the old adobe house on Dupont street, familiarly known as the *casa grande,* and are grading the ground on which it stood to a level with the street. This is the last building but one now remaining that was built before the discovery of gold, when San Francisco was a small village and her population but a few hundreds.

The disastrous conflagrations that have visited our city have swept [away] every vestige of the industry and enterprise of the primitive inhabitants, but by a train of fortuitous circumstances, the old adobe witnessed all and yet remained unscathed. The severe rain storms of the last winter have told with injurious effect upon the stability of its structure, and prudence dictates that it should be leveled with the ground, for fear that it may suddenly fall and overwhelm the neighbors in its ruins.

This is a fast and progressive age; and though such buildings were well suited for the times in which they were built, and though at the present time its history is linked with a thousand pleasant and interesting reminiscences and associations, the spirit of the age demands that it should be supplanted by a larger and a better structure. It has seen San Francisco rise from a few fishing hamlets to a city of great commercial wealth and importance; has seen the greater portion of it repeatedly laid in ashes, and as often rebuilt with renewed splendor and elegance; and is now forced to give way before the irresistible march of improvement.

The day of gay and merry fandangos is over—the music that once resounded through its halls is hushed—the happy groups that once assembled there have parted forever; its glory has disappeared at the presence of the Anglo-Saxon, and nothing now is left of the old adobe, except as part of the history of the commercial emporium of the Pacific.

Index